GW01425146

JUST A LITTLE CHARITY

A Social History

JUST A LITTLE CHARITY

A Social History

JOHN WOLTERS

PHILLIMORE

2006

Published by
PHILLIMORE & CO. LTD
Shopwyke Manor Barn, Chichester, West Sussex, England
www.phillimore.co.uk

© John Wolters, 2006
The right of John Wolters to be identified as the author of this work has been
asserted by him in accordance with the Copyright, Designs and Patents Act, 1988

All rights reserved. No part of this publication may be reproduced or transmitted
in any form or by any means, electronic, mechanical, photocopying, recording
or otherwise without the prior written permission of the Publishers or a
licence permitting restricted copying from the Copyright Licensing Agency Ltd,
90 Tottenham Court Road, London, WIP 9HE.

This book is sold subject to the condition that it shall not, by way of trade or
otherwise, be lent, resold, hired out, or otherwise circulated without the Publishers'
prior consent in any form of binding or cover than that in which it is published
and without a similar condition including this condition being imposed on the
subsequent purchaser.

ISBN 1-86077-398-2
ISBN 13 978-1-86077-398-3

Printed and bound in Great Britain by
THE CROMWELL PRESS
Trowbridge, Wiltshire

Coronae Meae et Gaudio

Conjugi Carissimae

Animo Gratissimo

Contents

List of Illustrations

Acknowledgements

I am most grateful to the following for permission to use material herein and their help: The Lord Bishop of London; The Lord Bishop of Chester; The Lord Bishop of Chichester; The Dean and Chapter of Hereford and the Hereford Mappa Mundi Trust; The Right Honourable Lord Baker, CH; The Revd Professor W.O. Chadwick, OM, KMPG.

Also, the late Dr David Newsome; The Governors and Headmasters of the following schools: Charterhouse; City of London; Eton College; Harrow; The King's School, Canterbury; Marlborough College; Merchant Taylors'; Rugby; St Paul's; Uppingham; Wellington College; The Warden and Scholars of Winchester College; The Archivists of the above schools; Eton College Photographic Archive; The Curator of the Royal Military College Sandhurst; Independent Association of Preparatory Schools; Brian Manning, Head of Art at Tonbridge School; The London Library; Schoolmistresses and Governesses Benevolent Institution; Bedford and Luton Archives Department; Whitby Archives Heritage Centre; *Scarborough Evening News* (14 December 1914); *The Times* (10 January 1806; 20 December 1808; 23 December 1816; 2 February 1822; 1 January 1828; 21 December 1836; October 1866; 22 December 1882; 3 December 1891; 5 October 1895); Batsford Limited.

Preface

In 1831 an entry in the Relief Book reads 'lunatic formerly a schoolmaster'. The idea for this work comes from another 'lunatic' who thought at a dinner that the history of this little-known charity, the Society of Schoolmasters and Schoolmistresses, should be written. It has been a rewarding task and what I thought might be a pamphlet has turned out to be something rather more substantial.

The history of the Society is a very human one. The needs of those the Charity was set up to help are the same today, almost in spite of the welfare state. The hopes and ambitions of its Committee are also natural ones. Of course, mistakes were made in its history, which spans more than 200 years – over-optimism, a failure to maintain the impetus when things were going well, a touch of arrogance here, of complacency there – such things are to be expected of a group of men and women who were and are true amateurs, working for no reward at the same time as performing their regular jobs in what has become an increasingly professional area of expertise. What is also clear is how very difficult it is for charities, large and small, to squeeze support from people and organisations who are thought to be natural allies. Charities such as this Society rely all too much for their financial well-being, and thus their ability to help those in need, on the very few. The saviour in the case of this Society has almost certainly been Eton College.

Where primary source material has been included, I have retained the spelling, grammar and punctuation as it is recorded. There are a wealth of case histories from which to select such evidence; I have chosen those which appear to me to be the most interesting and which fall within certain groupings. I hope that it does not appear too much of a catalogue.

I would like to thank the several people who have helped me in the compilation of this work. Firstly, I am grateful to the Society of Schoolmasters and Schoolmistresses for allowing me access to the Records of the Society and to quote from them. May I also thank Heather Wolters for her constant advice, encouragement and patience; David and Clare Wormald for their help in putting the material together, which in Clare's case has been beyond the call of duty; David Skipper for his initial suggestion, without which this would not have been written, and for his subsequent help; John Clark at Eton; the late Stanley Smith for his overall knowledge of the Society and, in particular, for providing information on the *Crown and Anchor* tavern where it all began. My thanks are also due to John Smalman-Smith, Canon Keith Wilkinson, Dr Roger Mallion, John Davison and all the Committee, Geoff and Lynn Springett, and John and Pippa Scorer for information and research. I am much indebted to Roddy Forman for his invaluable help in reading the text and for his suggestions, and to Mark Phillips at Eton for his support in ways which have gone beyond the selection of photographs. To all of them and anyone I've inadvertently missed out, my grateful appreciation.

All profits from the sale of this book will be given to the Charity.

Foreword

I am very grateful for the enthusiastic way in which John Wolters has taken up the idea, mooted towards the end of a splendid dinner in the Charteris Room at Eton, of recording the history of our Society. The dinner marked our recent partnership with the Schoolmistresses and Governesses Benevolent Institution, the latest development in the evolution of a charity which, small though it is, still functions effectively after more than 200 years.

Painstaking research has produced an account spanning a period of remarkable change, not least in the nation's view of both education and an employer's responsibility to its less fortunate employees. All this, and more besides, is mirrored in a readable and amusing narrative, the sort of book you can enjoy dipping into.

The Society acknowledges the support given by the late Tim Card, one-time Vice-Provost of Eton, and his family, as well as that of the Mercers' Company, without whose help this book would not have been possible.

David Skipper
President, Society of Schoolmasters and Schoolmistresses

Abbreviations

COS	Charity Organisation Society
DGAA	Distressed Gentlefolks Aid Association
GS	Grammar School
HMC	Headmasters' Conference
IAAM	Incorporated Association of Assistant Masters
IAPS	Independent Association of Preparatory Schools
Life Fund	The Life Fund is also known as the Joint Stock Fund. I have referred to it as the former throughout
PCAC	Professional Classes Aid Council
SGBI	Schoolmistresses and Governesses Benevolent Institution
SOS	Society of Schoolmasters
SOSS	Society of Schoolmasters and Schoolmistresses (from 1997)
The Society	As above
The Committee	The Committee of the Society of Schoolmasters and Schoolmistresses

Introduction

Private charities in the 18th and 19th centuries were very important in the relief of poverty. Such charities were devoted to many different causes – relief of widows, schoolmasters, the sick, blind, deaf and crippled, and the education of poor children – but they lacked overall organisation. Hence they were rather haphazard affairs, and charities found it difficult to respond to changing social or political circumstances. Several charities were very small and narrow in their objectives and their administrations were local to their immediate area. Charity-giving, which had fallen off at the start of the 18th century, was given a boost by the Evangelical Revival: William Wilberforce gave away a quarter of his income and supported some seventy philanthropic organisations, one of which was the Society of Schoolmasters (SOS). It has been estimated that at the start of the 19th century private charities were disbursing about £4 million a year. Sampson Low's analysis of London charities suggests that there were 114 in the capital before 1800, that a further 279 were founded in the next 50 years, and that by 1862 there were 640. These received £1.6 million in voluntary donations in 1860, which compares favourably with Poor Law spending in 1857 of £1.4 million. In the late 1860s charitable expenditure in London was between £5.5 and £7 million a year. The Poor Box at Marylebone Police Court raised £306, a sum used to provide 2,000 applicants with coal, soup and bread.

It was in order to overcome the lack of overall organisation that the Society for Organising Charitable Relief and Repressing Mendicity, usually known as the Charity Organisation Society (COS), was set up. SOS worked with it under both its names. COS had been established to check on the worthiness of applicants and avoid waste and duplication; in this way it was to help the Poor Law function more effectively. The man behind COS was C.S. Loch, a young Scot who was inspired by the work of the early 19th-century minister, Thomas Chalmers, who had tried to establish a scheme of help in the urban environment of his parish in Glasgow. As a result of Loch's skills, COS's reputation spread far and wide and by 1891 he was in touch with 75 similar organisations. While COS was unpopular with the poor, who did not like the checks imposed, it made the general public far more aware of the general problems associated with poverty and, by concentrating on individual cases, it pioneered casework and was, therefore, the 'parent of modern social work' (Edward

Royle). While Loch may, rightly, stand accused of failing to respond to greater state intervention at the start of the 20th century and hindering COS's modernisation as a result, such was his contribution and that of COS to family casework that it was renamed the Family Welfare Association in 1946.

By then, of course, the state had taken over the responsibilities that private charities had shouldered for so long. This it did largely through increasing direct taxation, and ever since the state began playing this leading role donations to private charities have fallen away and special appeals, rather than regular subscriptions and donations, have had to be relied upon.

It is in no way surprising that the Society of Schoolmasters' history mirrors these developments; it also reflects the view that both Beveridge (1942) and the Nathan Committee on Charitable Trusts (1952) took – that the welfare state would not make private charities unnecessary. The voluntary effort has indeed remained essential, so much so that the number of registered charities in Britain between 1979 and 1984 increased by 17,000, bringing the total to 150,000; the top 200 had a total income of £950 million in 1984. And this was at a time which had seen living standards rise significantly – 1953-73 saw the real incomes of the poorest five to ten per cent of the population increase by nearly seventy-five per cent.

So who needed all this aid? In the late 18th and early 19th centuries, it is estimated that at any one time between one third and one half of the total population were living in poor housing, ill-clothed, undernourished and on an inadequate income. While the effects of old age, illness and the death of the breadwinner hit all classes, it is likely that manual workers were the most vulnerable; all who were reduced by such circumstances became dependent on Christian charities. Pauperism is not an exact science: it hit different parts of the country at different times as wages and prices fluctuated – sometimes, as between 1780 and 1850, wildly. Certain periods do stand out, however, and affected much of the country: the inflation that accompanied the French and Napoleonic wars, the economic problems of 1920-2 and the Depression years following the Wall Street Crash of 1929 are just three examples.

Even if it appears relatively easy to generalise, the debate on living standards remains difficult and often misleading. In his monumental *Life and Labour of the People of London*, published between 1889 and 1903, Charles Booth took the level of income as the basis of his division of the population into eight categories. Category B represented those in irregular work, the very poor; those in Category C (the poor) had intermittent earnings of between 18s. and 21s. a week; those of the upper middle class who kept servants fell into Category H. The 1911 Census divided the population along five occupational lines: I represented the professionals, II the intermediate occupations, IV the partly skilled. It is not easy to place out-of-work schoolmasters or their ushers! Indeed, teaching, along with journalism, had only been recognised as an occupational category in 1861, an event which raised teachers' status, but only up to a point – a great gulf remained between the mere schoolteacher and the schoolmaster or schoolmistress. The former was seen as being lower middle-class and enjoyed little respect, whereas the latter taught middle-class children in middle-class schools and, as is seen from membership of the Society, often enjoyed high personal status in any case. What is clear, as Seebohm Rowntree showed for York, is that people who fell into Booth's B or C categories, for whatever reasons and from whatever heights, needed their income to be supplemented.

In the 1820s William Cobbett estimated that £1 4s. a week was needed to keep a family of five in bread, meat and beer (the average size of a family, 4.75, altered little between 1600 and 1900). Meat was a bit optimistic, for as Kay-Shuttleworth showed in his 1832 study of cotton workers, many of the poor had to survive on a diet of white bread, porridge, oatmeal, potatoes, a little fat bacon and not much else. Meat was rare, and as one worker said in 1849, 'Lor' bless you, we shouldn't know ourselves if we got meat'. Besides, many workers could not reach Cobbett's target – let alone those out of work. In the 1830s an agricultural worker in Wiltshire received less than 10s. and a handloom weaver in Oldham took home 7s. It also depended on where you lived: in 1825 a carpenter would earn 17s. a week in Glasgow, but in Manchester 24s. and in Greenwich 30s. A London compositor on a morning paper in the 1830s earned a princely 48s. a week. Regional differences were accentuated between 1879 and 1913, a period during which the agricultural labourer became far worse off than his urban counterpart as the price of wheat and land fell and competition from abroad grew. Cobbett's £1 4s. had become £1 0s. 6d. but only five counties in England achieved this. Poverty remained a huge problem – and not just in rural areas. In 1891 it was calculated that about ten per cent (400,000) of London's inhabitants were on casual or irregular earnings; in Oldham as many as forty-one per cent might be below the poverty line in a bad year, and Rowntree's studies in York showed that 15.4 per cent of the working class were in poverty in 1899.

It is also true that real wages for some rose between 1870 and 1895 by about forty-five per cent and that during the 20th century things slowly improved as unemployment fell from its peak of 2.7 million in 1932. For those in good work things certainly seemed better: by 1910 a male industrial worker could earn £75 per annum, while for a middle-class man the average annual salary was £340. Yet in 1938 22 million workers earned less than £125 a year and in 1955 the same group received £510 – though real incomes had gone up by 24 per cent.

It was believed that after 1945 poverty had been conquered – Rowntree's third survey of York (1950) showed that only 1.7 per cent of the population were living in poverty and that the main causes had been reduced to old age and illness – and it is true that poverty by 18th- and 19th-century standards has virtually disappeared. But, as Beveridge and Nathan have indicated, the welfare state will not eradicate poverty and this is something that the history of the Society of Schoolmasters confirms.

1

Beginnings

On 12 January 1797, a number of boarding schoolmasters made their way down a busy and noisy Strand, passing the several theatres, restaurants, coffee houses, playing-card makers, saddlers and pavement artists ('screevers'). They may have noticed outside number 30 the placards advertising 'Warrens Blacking', the place where Dickens was later to work as a child. They may even have seen, as Dickens was to see so often, the familiar figure of a bent-double lady, then of course younger, groping her way along the Strand's wide, well-paved street. If they had come from the south of the river, they would have had to cross the Thames by either London or Westminster Bridge or by boat, for Waterloo Bridge, the most convenient way over for their destination, was not completed until 1817. If they came from the north or east, they may have hurried through Covent Garden and Drury Lane and its miserable warren of narrow streets that housed its notorious gambling clubs, brothels and gin shops. (At the beginning of the 19th century about 25,000 Londoners were arrested for drunkenness, some by Fielding's Bow Street Runners.) Coming from the north-west, they may have passed through the fashionable squares and roads of Mayfair and Kensington, which had been developed in the second half of the 18th century as London expanded and reached a population of one million in 1800 – a population that would continue to grow by 20 per cent in each of the next five decades, remarkable considering that baptisms had first exceeded deaths in London only in 1790. The Strand may have been one of London's better streets but it was in some ways similar to Covent Garden – the *Talbot* and *Fountain* inns were well-known homosexual haunts and if one had asked directions to the Strand, one would almost certainly have been directed by pubs. Prostitutes plied their trade and the area was not a place to linger at night – gas lighting of the Strand did not arrive until the 1840s – but on the whole it was not too off-putting. Many people worked in Somerset House and the Admiralty; Jane Austen's brother, Henry, lived above the offices of his banking house in Henrietta Street and Jane often stayed there, frequenting the local dress shops; Charles and Mary Lamb lived in Russell Street, where they entertained Keats, Coleridge, Southey, Leigh Hunt, Hazlitt and Wordsworth, who wrote 'On Westminster Bridge' in 1802.

The destination of these schoolmasters was a well-known centre for political and social meetings, the *Crown and Anchor* tavern. The tavern stood on the corner of

1   *The* Crown and Anchor *tavern to the right of St Clement Danes in the Strand.*

the Strand and Arundel Street. It was 'a large and curious house, with good rooms and other conveniences fit for entertainments'.[1] It was no stranger to the famous and influential: Johnson and Boswell had often dined there, as had Sir Joshua Reynolds. It was the venue for meetings of the Academy of Antient Music and it was where Sidney Smith's brother 'Bobus' Smith instituted the 'King of Clubs'. Pitt the Younger came to the *Crown and Anchor* as a member of the Western Circuit Club, and it was from the *Crown and Anchor* that Edmund Burke wrote his last letter to Mrs Crewe on 21 May 1797. In this letter he deplored the days in which he lived, commenting that 'the club at the Crown and Anchor [is] not one jot less treasonable than the Committee at Belfast; and what is worse the names are higher, and the members of Parliament openly show themselves here'.[2]

It was here that the schoolmasters held a meeting that led to the formation of the Society of Schoolmasters. That they were there at all was the result of an idea believed to have emerged from Eton, though the precise details are sketchy. Predominantly clerical and wealthy, young to middle-aged, living and working in London and the south east, they were to use the *Crown and Anchor* for their meetings until 1824; it was a place where they would have felt entirely at home. At this meeting they elected a Committee under the chairmanship of the Revd Dr Barrow, Headmaster of the Soho Academy in Soho Square to which Boswell had sent his son. The object of the Society (initially called an Association) was to further the interests of the teaching profession and it was the first organisation of its kind. By the end of their first meeting, the Committee had set itself three tasks and given itself a year to find out how to achieve them. The challenge was not an easy one: firstly, how might the widows and children of deceased schoolmasters and schoolmasters unable to continue because of 'age, infirmity or other misfortune'[3] best be helped; secondly, how could the most advantageous terms for books and stationery for the teaching profession be obtained; and, thirdly, how might the profession 'most easily assist masters of ability and reputation'?[4] These are questions that many would still like answered.

There can be little doubt about the need for such a society. Apart from the nine ancient public schools – Eton, Harrow, Winchester, Shrewsbury, Merchant Taylors', St Paul's, Westminster, Rugby and Charterhouse – which attracted great prestige, there was a host of grammar and small private schools. Many of these were poorly placed geographically to attract fee-paying pupils from the developing towns and cities of the 19th century, and so their Principals and their assistants (often a single usher) were vulnerable in a society increasingly seeking a more practical curriculum than the traditional diet of Classics. These men, for it was a masculine profession, were, like the

2   *Midas transmuting all into paper, 1797. Pitt is depicted by Gillray as a colossus controlling the money supply, though through the crown of notes on his head are the ears of an ass.*

rest of the population, exposed to the vagaries of disease and death, which could leave families not only devastated but without any form of state assistance, for there were no pensions, invalidity benefits or National Health Service. Such insurance schemes as existed were expensive – and that of the Society of Schoolmasters itself was hardly to be cheap. Politically, too, the turn of the century was a period of uncertainty and danger: Britain was at war with Revolutionary France and then Napoleon until 1815; the British royal family was the subject of scandal and ridicule; industrial and agricultural change was taking place on an unprecedented scale as the age of steam power, improved communications and factories dawned; and there was considerable unrest and much poverty. Such conditions did not help schoolmasters.

While wrestling with its three objectives, the Committee got involved with another matter which it believed came within its broad brief of furthering the interests of the teaching profession. William Pitt the Younger, 'that astounding political phenomenon',[5] still only 37 and First Lord of the Treasury and Chancellor of the Exchequer since 1783, was anxious to introduce a bill which would increase Assessed Taxes. His reason was simple: the French war had led to a run on gold in February 1797 and Pitt had ordered the Bank of England to cease issuing gold and issue notes instead.* The Committee of Schoolmasters was concerned at the effect any tax increase would have on boarding schools and sought to persuade Pitt to allow relief.

Accordingly, the Committee meeting at the *Crown and Anchor* on 6 December 1797 decided that Barrow should write to Pitt expressing the Society's concern at

---

*   In 1799 Pitt introduced Income Tax to finance the war.

T O SCHOOLMASTERS.—Any Gentleman in
want of a Capital House for a BOARDING SCHOOL,
may be furnished with one at a fair price, either to rent or purchase ; there are two acres of land attached to it, and a few
Pupils who will be given gratis to the tenant, who may be ca-
pable of the undertaking, or a young man who can procure a
few boarders, and who is in an age of activity, will be admitted
as partner, upon very easy terms, and after a few years, may
succeed to the business.   Applications may be made, by
writing (post paid) to X. Y. Z, at Mr. Young's, Broker, Lum-
ber-street, Seven Dials.   Personal application will not be attended to, nor any, but such as contain the real name and
abode of the writer.   The distance from town is two miles.

3   The Times, 10 January 1806: advertisements such as this were not uncommon and often hid the
problems associated with the position.

the hardship to which the profession would be subjected by the proposed tax, and
to solicit 'relief as he [Pitt] may judge not incompatible with the public service.'[6] Pitt,
replying the same evening, agreed to a meeting at 12.30pm the next day. On that
morning, Barrow sent Pitt a letter outlining the schoolmasters' case, being 'sensible of
the value of your time'. Barrow wrote that 'schoolmasters lived in large houses with an
extraordinary number of windows'[7] – a reference to the Window Tax, introduced in
1696 and not abolished until 1851 – and any new tax would place 'an undue sum on
them as they would be rated as high as many men of wealth'.[8] He went on to argue that
profits were low, fees could not be increased without risking loss of pupils and that
fees were in any case a problem for many parents. He suggested that schoolmasters
should be treated for tax purposes in the same way as 'inn and lodging house keepers.'[9]
He assured Pitt that his profession had no wish to escape from their responsibilities
and least of all during 'the ardent and important contest in which [we are] at present
engaged', and that they had not promoted their views through public meetings 'lest it
seem an encouragement to disaffected opposition from other bodies of men.'[10]

At the meeting Pitt was not unsympathetic, but argued that schoolmasters, and
others, 'should consider their income to be net of all necessary expenses for their
school and that a schoolmaster was not obliged to declare precisely what his income
was, but only that it did not exceed a certain sum.'[11] His response to objections that
the schoolmaster might find himself near to poverty as a result of this tax was to
ask Barrow and Hewlett,* who were representing the Association, what relief they
would suggest, how they would achieve it and for whom. Barrow and Hewlett could
only reply that relief should be given to *bona fide* schoolmasters who kept a school,
but 'neither carriages, horses, nor more than one manservant' and had neither 'private
property nor preferment in the Church'. Pitt gave this response scant attention,
dismissing their suggestions as 'ineffectual … offering equal relief to men with very

---

*   See Appendix II.

unequal claims.'[12] Instead Pitt urged Barrow and the Committee to think about a new idea: that of taxing men according to the number of pupils they had. He offered either to see them again or receive their views in writing, though these would have to be 'expressed by Monday next as the Bill would go to the Committee early in the week'.[13] The schoolmasters took the latter course and wrote a long letter (since lost) urging Pitt to tax schools along the lines he had asked them to consider, and detailed a plan for this purpose. The Act did not include this plan, but the Committee was more than satisfied that Pitt had 'granted the relief we requested in the same manner and to the full extent of what we wished and suggested'. Lobbying at the end of the 18th century obviously could have some effect! This also suggests that the Committee had some influence.

Reports of the meeting with Pitt were circulated before the General Meeting of 18 January 1798, though the main business concerned the Committee report on the three areas with which they had been charged. It was agreed that little progress could be made on how to obtain better staff until the Society was better established. As for books and stationery, various quotations had been obtained from 'booksellers of credit,'* and from these Messrs Rivingtons of St Paul's Church Square emerged as the best for books, and Richardson and Harrison of Leadenhall Street for stationery. Both demanded a list of members of the Association, who alone would be eligible for the rates they offered, and they wanted their accounts settled within six months. There is every indication that these arrangements worked well.

The major part of the Committee's report clearly concerned how to help those who had fallen on hard times. Their solution was a two-part Plan. The first was to raise, by subscriptions and benefactions, what amounted to a Life Assurance Fund (also known as a Joint Stock Fund) from which members and their dependants might benefit in line with the length of their membership. Subscribers had to be masters at endowed or boarding schools and claims could be made only after four years' subscription had been paid. Rates[14] were quite high: five guineas per annum and, for those joining the scheme over 40, an additional one guinea for each year by which they exceeded that age was payable. Benefactions were not restricted to schoolmasters, and those who gave over 20 guineas were entitled to become Officers of the Society, for this was the title that was now adopted. Members had to prove their *bona fides* by producing two certificates, one 'from the parish register or something similar'[15] to establish their age, the other from 'two medical persons of repute or two existing members of the Society'[16] to vouch for their health. New members could be admitted only at Annual General Meetings, and then only as a result of a ballot. The monies subscribed were to be handled and invested by bankers William Fuller and Chattris, and on the death of a subscriber who had fulfilled the regulations, the widow or orphans received a fixed sum.

The second part consisted of an Address to the public written by Barrow, appealing for the support of impecunious schoolmasters and their dependants through the

---

* Booksellers had congregated in and around St Paul's Churchyard since the 17th century, just as other tradesmen had their 'areas' – such as opticians in Ludgate Street, dentists in St Martin's Lane and butchers in Smithfield.

Committee.

STANDING ORDERS.

I. --- IT IS ORDERED, THAT as foon as the Chair is taken, the Minutes of the laft Meeting are to be read by the Chairman.

II. —THAT every Motion, which any Member intends to make in a Committee, with a view to its being fubmitted to the Society at the General Meeting, fhall be delivered in writing to the Chairman, in the courfe of the firft half hour, after the Chair is taken; and that all Motions, which are not fo delivered, fhall be referved, till the next Meeting; and fhall then be determined, in the order, in which they were offered, previous to the introduction of any new Motion.

III. —THAT the Chairman fhall not put the Queftion on any Motion, which has not been feconded.

IV. — THAT in the Debate on any Motion, no Member fhall be allowed to fpeak more than twice, except the Mover, who may claim the privilege of rifing a third time.

V. — THAT in the Debate on any Motion, the Member, who fpeaks, muft ftand up, and addrefs himfelf to the Chair; and that the reft of the Members prefent muft remain filent.

VI. — THAT when two or more Members rife together, the Chairman fhall determine which is to fpeak firft; and if the Speaker does not confine himfelf to the Motion before the Committee, the Chairman muft call him to order.

VII. --- THAT the Names of the Committee, who attend the Meetings, be noted by the Secretary.

VIII. — THAT on thofe Days, on which the Committee dine together, no motion or bufinefs whatever relative to the affairs of the Society fhall be brought before the Committee, after dinner.

IX. --- THAT on every Committee Day, a Copy of the Motions, which have been propofed, feconded and carried, fhall be delivered to the Secretary, figned by the Chairman, by the Mover and by the Seconder; in order that a full and proper record be entered on the annals of the Society; and be prefented to the confideration of the Members at large, on the day of the annual and general Meeting.

4   *Standing Orders 1799: the Society begins to get off the ground.*

setting up of a Charitable Fund. The Address stated the grounds for seeking public support by affirming the contribution made by the profession to society. 'Every man is what his education has made him,' wrote Barrow, who stressed:

> the arduousness of the task, the irksomeness of the incessant labour of the mind [in order] to fulfil with fidelity and reputation the charge undertaken ... The master finds a new task in every pupil – a different temper to be disciplined to habits of industry and virtue or different talents to be directed to their proper object.

The effect of all this industry was to 'exhaust the powers of body and mind'. The schoolmaster had chosen his lot but his 'recompense in general appears to be disproportionate and insufficient', especially when compared 'with emoluments available in other professions'. Fees were low and profits were small: 'he that polishes the manners only frequently obtains in a few hours, more than be procured in as many months, by him who impresses upon the mind the elements of useful science, and the doctrines and precepts of Christianity; the honourable gains of a merchant in a single year, will exceed what can be realised in a school by the labour and economy of the longest life'. For the widows and children of schoolmasters, Barrow continued, there was no provision, unlike in other professions which made public appeals similar to that envisaged by the Society. While the style may be a little different, the sentiments expressed in 1798 are still much in evidence in the 21st century.

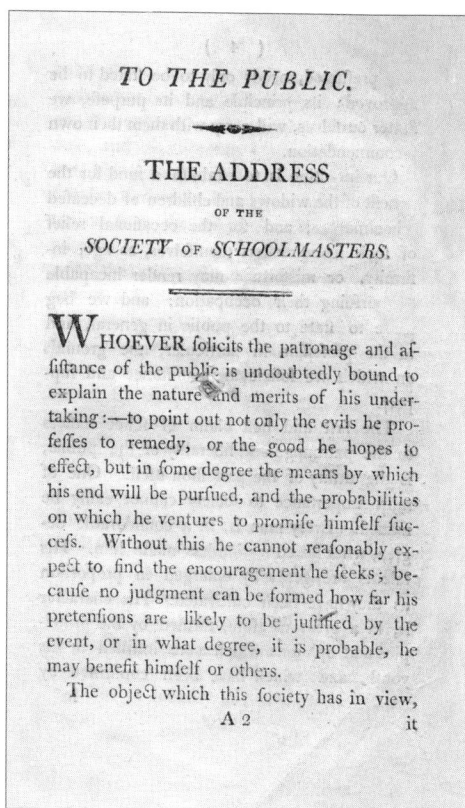

5 *Barrow's Address to the Public, 1798. Barrow was the first Chairman.*

The Annual General Meeting approved the report, resolutions and the Address, and agreed that Barrow should continue to chair a Committee of nine which would meet quarterly – something the Society continued to do until 1977, when this was reduced to three meetings a year. The Committee elected in 1798 in effect gave the Society three years to get off the ground. It set targets for numbers of subscribers and benefactors, for standing orders and rules to be formulated and for details of the two funds to be finalised. The plan for these was deemed very workable by no less an authority than the Equitable Assurance Office, whose advice the Society continued to seek; problems came when there was too much tinkering with the basic scheme – which occurred all too soon.

The Society's standing orders of 1799 demanded a noon start for the Annual General Meeting which had to be over by 4pm, at which time subscriptions and benefactions would be collected. This was so that dinner could be on the table by

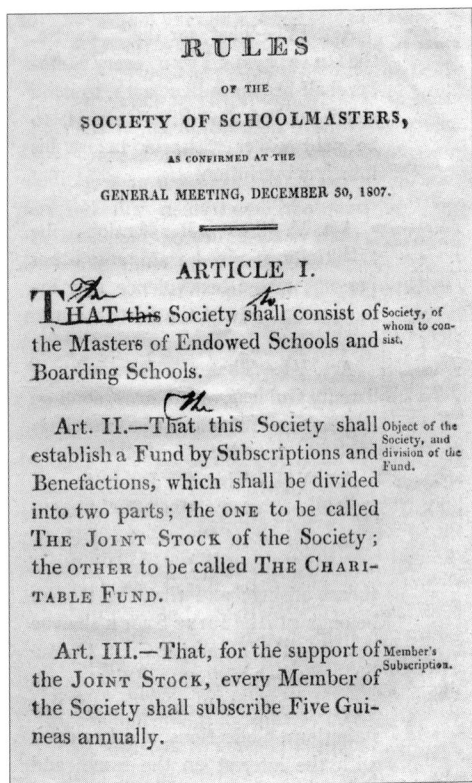

RULES

OF THE

SOCIETY OF SCHOOLMASTERS,

AS CONFIRMED AT THE

GENERAL MEETING, DECEMBER 30, 1807.

ARTICLE I.

THAT this Society shall consist of Society, of whom to consist. the Masters of Endowed Schools and Boarding Schools.

Art. II.—That this Society shall Object of the Society, and division of the Fund. establish a Fund by Subscriptions and Benefactions, which shall be divided into two parts; the ONE to be called THE JOINT STOCK of the Society; the OTHER to be called THE CHARITABLE FUND.

Art. III.—That, for the support of Member's Subscription. the JOINT STOCK, every Member of the Society shall subscribe Five Guineas annually.

6   *The Rules of the Life Fund, 1799.*

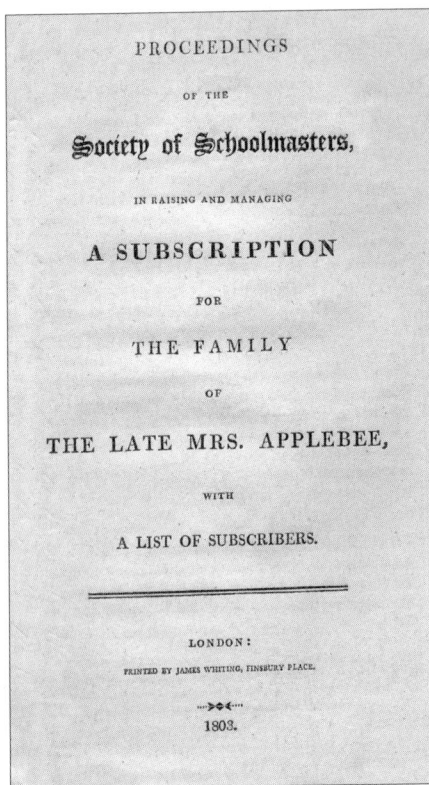

PROCEEDINGS

OF THE

Society of Schoolmasters,

IN RAISING AND MANAGING

A SUBSCRIPTION

FOR

THE FAMILY

OF

THE LATE MRS. APPLEBEE,

WITH

A LIST OF SUBSCRIBERS.

LONDON:

PRINTED BY JAMES WHITING, FINSBURY PLACE.

1803.

7   *The Applebee case needed urgent measures and led to an appeal in 1803.*

5pm.* The bill for this meal was to be brought to the Chairman at 7pm precisely, and from the amounts charged the members did not eat badly! Unless there was a debate on a motion, no one was allowed to speak more than once – and if there was no debate, the motion was deemed carried and binding. Speakers had to address the Chairman standing and no irrelevance was tolerated.

The 38 Rules of the Society were in place by 1801. These formally established the two funds, with subscriptions being placed in the Life (or Joint Stock) Fund and benefactions in the Charitable Fund. In 1802 the first Auditors' report offered some practical advice in order to achieve greater clarity – subscribers should be listed alphabetically with the sum subscribed alongside the name, and audited accounts should be produced every four years. Today we would like greater information about the men who became members but, for the most part, we have to make do with their names, ages and town or city of origin. Thus by 1801 the Society had met the targets set in 1798, including those of membership. Since 1799 it had had a new Chairman, the Revd Dr Charles Burney,† a distinguished schoolmaster, eminent Grecian and

---

*   Dinner in the late 18th century was taken between 3 and 5pm and this practice lasted into the 1830s.
†   See Appendix II.

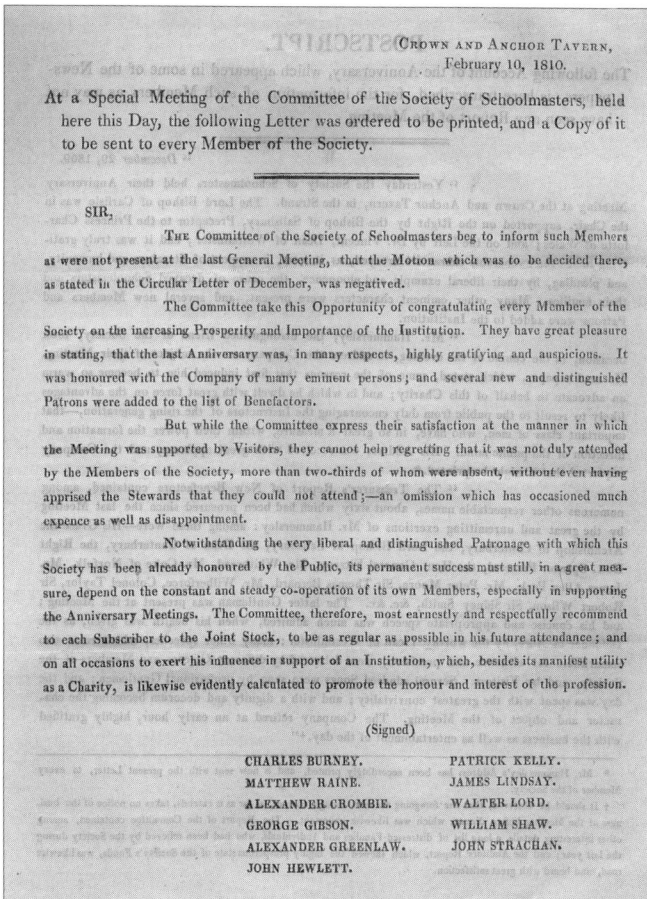

> CROWN AND ANCHOR TAVERN,
> February 10, 1810.
>
> At a Special Meeting of the Committee of the Society of Schoolmasters, held here this Day, the following Letter was ordered to be printed, and a Copy of it to be sent to every Member of the Society.
>
> SIR,
>
> THE Committee of the Society of Schoolmasters beg to inform such Members as were not present at the last General Meeting, that the Motion which was to be decided there, as stated in the Circular Letter of December, was negatived.
>
> The Committee take this Opportunity of congratulating every Member of the Society on the increasing Prosperity and Importance of the Institution. They have great pleasure in stating, that the last Anniversary was, in many respects, highly gratifying and auspicious. It was honoured with the Company of many eminent persons; and several new and distinguished Patrons were added to the list of Benefactors.
>
> But while the Committee express their satisfaction at the manner in which the Meeting was supported by Visitors, they cannot help regretting that it was not duly attended by the Members of the Society, more than two-thirds of whom were absent, without even having apprised the Stewards that they could not attend;—an omission which has occasioned much expence as well as disappointment.
>
> Notwithstanding the very liberal and distinguished Patronage with which this Society has been already honoured by the Public, its permanent success must still, in a great measure, depend on the constant and steady co-operation of its own Members, especially in supporting the Anniversary Meetings. The Committee, therefore, most earnestly and respectfully recommend to each Subscriber to the Joint Stock, to be as regular as possible in his future attendance; and on all occasions to exert his influence in support of an Institution, which, besides its manifest utility as a Charity, is likewise evidently calculated to promote the honour and interest of the profession.
>
> (Signed)
>
> CHARLES BURNEY.   PATRICK KELLY.
> MATTHEW RAINE.   JAMES LINDSAY.
> ALEXANDER CROMBIE.   WALTER LORD.
> GEORGE GIBSON.   WILLIAM SHAW.
> ALEXANDER GREENLAW.   JOHN STRACHAN.
> JOHN HEWLETT.

8 *Letter from Committee to members reminding them of the need to support the Society, 1810.*

brother of Madame D'Arblay.* Barrow had retired outside London. Burney and his son were to serve the Society in several capacities until 1863, beginning a tradition of long service by Committee members which has continued until this day.

Still in its infancy, the Society was not in any position to deal with emergencies, something demonstrated by the Applebee case of 1802, which forced the Committee to adopt special methods to meet the particular circumstances. Applebee was an original subscriber in 1798 and the first to signify approval of the 1801 Rules. He was Principal of Putney School but had fled to avoid his creditors, leaving his wife and six children homeless and destitute and forced to take refuge in a public house in Chelsea. The situation having been reported to the Committee, immediate relief was sent, but Mrs Applebee was already dangerously ill. A physician was called but too

---

* Madame D'Arblay is probably better known as Fanny Burney (1752 - 1840), the novelist. Charles, her favourite brother, and she were among the children of Dr Charles Burney, himself a distinguished musicologist (d.1814). Her brother died in December 1818. In 1793 Fanny married General D'Arblay, a penniless liberal *émigré*.

late. This unfortunate woman expired in a few days, in a most deplorable state, both of body and mind; and must have been buried by the parish, had not the Committee take on the expense.'[17]

The Society now took responsibility for the children – four sons (aged 16, 15, nine and eight) and two girls aged 11 and three. Because the Society was hardly established and so unable to afford permanent relief to so large a family, it set up a separate subscription for them. This attracted wide support and raised the not inconsiderable sum of £405 2s. Contributors included the Bishop of Chester, the Marchioness of Downshire, Lord and Lady Kinnaird and the Lord Chief Justice, Ellenborough. The monies were invested, managed and administered by a sub-committee under Thomas Hammersley of Pall Mall, whose son was at Applebee's school and who was so moved by the situation that he became an important supporter of the Society. His committee found a situation in Jamaica for the eldest boy and kitted him out for £60; his 15-year-old brother was able to follow him later and Christ's Hospital took the younger boys. The oldest girl, Mary, was educated and kept by a member, the Revd William Carmalt, until she was thought old enough to be apprenticed* and the youngest daughter was supported from the fund which had been set up. In all, £90 was spent on 'various necessaries', £40 reserved for current expenses and the rest was invested. Nor was the family forgotten: in 1809 Dr Patrick Kelly,† Secretary and Treasurer to the Society, reported that 'the youngest son was about to leave the Blue Coat School, and being tolerably forward in classical education, a situation should be looked out for him. Dr Lindsay undertook to make an enquiry of a medical friend, who, he believed, wanted a youth of his description.[18]

Although this highlights the worst sort of problem the Society has had to deal with in its 200-year existence, the Applebee case brought benefit to the Society in the form of Thomas Hammersley. His support was both generous and influential and a charity working in very different educational circumstances needed all the support it could get if it were to meet the many calls on its funds.

---

*   Mary Applebee was apprenticed to 'a mantua making [dress maker] and millenary [sic] business' for three years. The Society paid the £30 apprentice fee. A mantua was a woman's loose gown.
†   See Appendix II.

2

A Little Over Confidence?

The Society entered the 19th century with some optimism. Its structures were in place, accounting systems were clarified and simplified, and application procedures were tightened. The Society also sought to improve its structure throughout the country, for there was a danger that it might become restricted largely to the south east. To this end, a system of area representatives was introduced; in time this spread to cover the country and, at its height, local representatives were supported by local committees. One of the first representatives was Arnold's predecessor at Rugby, the Revd Dr John Wooll, who, 'being very active in his area [was asked] to become agent for that area'.[1] Such men helped to promote the Society at the same time as identifying needy cases and checking credentials. With a developing administration, the Society appointed the Revd G. Gibson to act as Secretary to the Committee while Dr Kelly shouldered the burdens of being Secretary and Treasurer to the Society.

In London the Committee continued to defend the interests of schoolmasters by challenging the effects of the Window Tax in 1804; a deputation tackled Addington (later Viscount Sidmouth), the Prime Minister from 1801 to 1804. We do not have details of this meeting but it must have been held shortly before that sorry figure fell and Pitt returned, for the Minutes record that the deputation 'be requested to learn when they can wait on Mr Pitt'.[2] Window Tax was a subject the Society, and in particular Kelly, did not give up on: in 1817 they were concerned at rumoured changes to the Tax and took on Vansittart, Chancellor of the Exchequer, 1812-23, who allayed their fears by stating there 'was no intention to make any alteration to the present Window Tax'.[3]

Initially both the Life and Charitable Funds appeared to be working successfully. Membership and donations grew in these early years, so much so that the Committee could regularly report to its members 'the Committee congratulate you and themselves'[4] on this rising prosperity. They would have been wise to exercise a little more caution. For a time, nevertheless, things went well. The Life Fund paid out generously when called upon according to the number of subscriptions received – in 1809 William King's daughter got £160 on his death, King having contributed 11 subscriptions of five guineas. For the Fund to continue to be successful, however, contributors needed to outnumber claimants, and there was always a degree of unpredictability in this. The balance was made less easy to achieve by the high subscription rate – five guineas a year was a large sum for schoolmasters, and the result was that they were not queuing up to join. Indeed, one of the criticisms that can be levelled at the Fund is that its appeal was too limited and any confidence in its future was misplaced.

As for the Charitable Fund, it helped so many cases of hardship that in 1805 it was decided to limit the money given in relief to half the income received by the Fund in the previous year. Later this was increased to two-thirds. It was not easy for any charity to test the genuineness of the application and the Society was sorely tried in this respect. Some applicants were turned down on technical grounds, a few as being unsuitable. One such was Mr Nicholas Downing, a writer and mathematical assistant who 'having been in prison and his character not being satisfactory was judged inadmissible'.[5] But there were far more cases of real hardship, especially those of widows and widowers left destitute and with several children. The Revd George Nicholson of Hull, once a schoolmaster in Barking, Essex, was left with eight children and was, in any case, 'decayed'. The Revd William Harris of Sloane Street, London, a member for 10 years, had died intestate, leaving a wife and 'also by a former wife two daughters now residing in America'.[6] Help was given in both cases. The Revd Richard Shields of Hampstead was one of the first and most active members. He was the first Secretary of what was then the Association and a Committee member until 1802. Soon after, he had 'become somewhat deranged in his mind, had left his home for more than three months and had not been heard of, and his family was in great distress'.[7] In this case, the Society contributed five guineas to a subscription fund set up by his friends. A similar solution was arrived at for Mrs French of Bow, whose husband had died very suddenly, leaving her pregnant and with eight other children 'in afflictive circumstances without means of adequate support'.[8] A Mrs Townsend, a widow from St Pancras, was already receiving relief when 'a daughter burnt to death and this [not surprisingly] had occasioned great injury to her health'.[9] She received an extra two guineas.

These were typical cases and well worthy of the Charitable Fund's support. The Committee, however, occasionally erred on the side of generosity, as it did with the persistent John Field, who had reapplied in 1808. Field was 'an aged schoolmaster who claimed continuing indigent circumstances' and was given four guineas on the promise 'that he would never again apply to the Society for relief'.[10]

If the Society were really to achieve its objectives however, meetings with Prime Ministers and the introduction of new systems counted for little. What was needed was money. The Society could not survive for ever on an ageing membership: the Life Fund needed an influx of younger members and the Charitable Fund needed donations. For many years the Annual Dinner had been a profitable source of money, supplementing the initial enthusiasm for a new society. Dinners were held at the *Crown and Anchor* and attracted large numbers. They were advertised in the press and several papers carried reports in their columns. Diners were attracted by the presence of the royal princes – the Duke of Cambridge was the Society's Patron – for, perhaps surprisingly given the reputation of the royal family, people were keen to be seen in their company and to demonstrate, as well, their own charitable credentials. Thus the funds benefited.

Dinners were cheerful and lively affairs. In 1804 it was noted that 'the schoolmasters of London and its vicinity had a great dinner today [20 December] in the room above us and were, by the noise they made, very joyous; Dr Huntingford, Bishop of Gloucester,* was in the Chair'.[11] When Burney took the Chair, he usually gave the toast, 'May the birch-tree never be supplanted by the tree of Liberty', and this led one founder member, the Revd William Jones, to comment, 'these sentiments particularly suited Dr Burney, for I have been repeatedly assured that the article "birch" is distinctly charged in all his school accounts, and that he buys it by the cartload'!'[12] Every dinner was accompanied by 'a series of rousing songs, "The Vacation", which were performed professionally, many to the tune of "The Roast Beef of Old England"' (see Appendix IV). Press reports in 1809 confirm this:

> Yesterday the Society of Schoolmasters held their Anniversary Meeting at the Crown and Anchor in the Strand. The Lord Bishop of Carlisle (Dr Goodenough)† was in the Chair, supported on the Right by the Bishop of Salisbury, Preceptor to the Princess Charlotte of Wales; and on the Left by Dr Vincent, Dean of Westminster;[13] and it was very gratifying to see these venerable characters arrayed, as it were, in support of literature and humanity, and pleading, by their liberal example and eloquence, the cause of decayed schoolmasters and their families … Several admired Songs were sung by professional Gentlemen; and the day was spent with the greatest conviviality; and with a dignity and decorum becoming the character and object of the Meeting. The Company retired at an early hour, highly gratified with the business as well as entertainment of the day.[14]

On Wednesday last the Anniversary Dinner of the Society of Schoolmasters was held at the Crown and Anchor Tavern, the Rev. Dr. RAINE, Head Master of the Charterhouse School, in the Chair. Notwithstanding the unfavourable state of the weather, which prevented many of the Country Members from attending, the Meeting was numerous, and the accession of new Subscribers considerable. The Report of the Committee stated various instances of the utility of the Institution, in affording, during the last year, much relief to distressed Schoolmasters and their families. Several interesting letters were received; and one in particular, from THOMAS HAMMERSLEY, Esq. excited much attention and regard. It contained several judicious observations on certain important objects which might be effected by the Society; and it besides contained a long list of Subscribers to this Charity, whom he had procured since the last Meeting. Among the toasts, the Memory of the late Professor PORSON was received with peculiar marks of sympathy and respect. It was given from the Chair in an affecting strain of eloquence; in the course of which, Dr. RAINE took occasion to observe, that learning had sustained an irreparable loss in the death of this great man, whom he described as one of the brightest ornaments of ancient literature that the world ever saw. He also touched with much tenderness on the long and uninterrupted friendship which had subsisted between him and Mr. PORSON; and he likewise greatly interested the feelings of the company by stating the zeal which the Greek Professor had always manifested for the success of the Society of Schoolmasters, and that, besides his annual subscription, he sent an additional and unexpected donation to this Charity, within a few days of his last illness. The day was spent, as usual, with great harmony. Messrs. DICKSON, TAYLOR, THOMSON, and other gentlemen of celebrity, favoured the Meeting with many excellent songs, some of which were composed for the occasion; and the company retired at an early hour, highly gratified with the business as well as the entertainment of the day.

On Friday night, a Gentleman, in passing the market-place of North Shields, missed his road, and got above the knees in snow, when a man sprung upon his back, and with the greatest dexterity picked his pocket of his gold watch, and escaped. He was, however, apprehended on Saturday night, when he confessed the theft, and gave intelligence where the watch was deposited. His reason for committing the act is rather curious, viz. *that he was weary of life.*

9 The Times *report of the Annual Dinner, 20 December 1808.*

One of those who was there was the Revd William Jones. Jones was first curate and then vicar of Broxbourne. His stipend as a curate was £20 a year and, finding this inadequate even in the 1790s, he started a school. This was evidently sufficiently successful for him to subscribe from the outset. Jones used to ride to London on horseback for meetings and his time for the journey is said to have been somewhat

---

*　See Appendix II.
†　See Appendix II.

10 *George Huntingford, Bishop of Gloucester and then Hereford, the first President.*

better than that of much public transport today. He was probably not a typical member, for he had 'an elm coffin made for him which he used to keep as a bookcase in his study but the good man had not thought of increasing corpulence and at his death the corpse could not be accommodated'![15]

For all its good intentions and outward confidence, the Society was in danger of running before it could properly walk and by 1809 the need for new members and more donations on a regular basis was becoming clear. Appeal was therefore made to the schools, to the public and to the wealthy and influential. The Address, this time written by Burney, was accompanied by a letter from a 'well-wisher' which had been put before the Annual Meeting. The Chairman, the Bishop of Carlisle, Goodenough, persuaded its author, Thomas Hammersley, to acknowledge it. Hammersley had already done much for the Society and in this letter he went further. He touched on the Life Fund, drawing attention to its benefits for schoolmasters and their families, but his main objective was to win support for the Charitable Fund. 'If this fund prospered,' he wrote,

> it would encourage teachers of distinguished merit and ability and from such teachers the country may expect better scholars, and improvement in morals, warmer in religion … and the people may proceed humbly to approach the Throne of Grace, and to supplicate the Almighty to look down upon them as a Nation, and be pleased to stretch out His Mighty Arm to save them, in their time of peril and necessity.

We might well express things rather differently today, but Hammersley went on to urge support and donations for the Society, and few would dispute this as being necessary.

POSTSCRIPT.

The following Account of the Anniversary, which appeared in some of the News-papers, is here transcribed, for the information of such Members as may not have seen any Report of the Meeting.

"*December 29, 1809.*

"Yesterday the Society of Schoolmasters held their Anniversary Meeting at the Crown and Anchor Tavern, in the Strand. The Lord Bishop of Carlisle was in the Chair, supported on the Right by the Bishop of Salisbury, Preceptor to the Princess Charlotte of Wales; and on the Left by Dr. Vincent, Dean of Westminster; and it was truly gratifying to see these venerable characters arrayed, as it were, in support of literature and humanity, and pleading, by their liberal example and eloquence, the cause of decayed Schoolmasters and their families. Many other eminent characters were present, and several new Members and Patrons were added to the Institution.

"Mr. Hammersley, the distinguished friend of the Society, took occasion, in the course of the evening, to address the Company on the subject of their Meeting. He read a paper, which stated, some of the reasons that first induced him to become so warm an advocate in behalf of this Charity; and in which he dwelt with great force on the advantages likely to result to the public from duly encouraging the Instructors of the rising generation,—that important class of men, who have, in so great a measure, within their power the formation and direction of the public mind. His Address was received with great applause, and the Company requested that it might be printed. *

"The Treasurer's Report of New Benefactors contained, among numerous other respectable names, about sixty which had been procured since the last Meeting by the great and unremitting exertions of Mr. Hammersley: among these were—His Grace the Archbishop of Canterbury, the Lord Bishop of Salisbury, the Dean of Canterbury, the Right Hon. Spencer Perceval, the Hon. General Fitzroy, Mr. Whitbread, Mr. Coke of Norfolk, Mr. James Allen Park, Mr. Peter Moore, Sir Thomas Bernard, Mr. Wilberforce, Colonel Taylor, Sir Robert Wilson, Sir Sidney Smith, &c. &c. The latter Gentleman was present at the Meeting; and his concise and appropriate speech was much admired, when his health was given, as the Defender of Acre, by the worthy Dean of Westminster: many other speeches, which were also remarkable for elegance and precision, were delivered by different Officers and Members of the Society, and by Visitors. Several admired Songs were sung by professional Gentlemen; and the day was spent with the greatest conviviality; and with a dignity and decorum becoming the character and object of the Meeting. The Company retired at an early hour, highly gratified with the business as well as entertainment of the day.†"

---

* Mr. Hammersley's Address has been accordingly printed, and is now sent with the present Letter, to every Member of the Society.

† It should be observed, that the foregoing account, though correct, as far as it extends, takes no notice of the business of the Meeting before dinner, which was likewise important. The Report of the Committee contained, among other interesting details, a long list of distressed Families and Individuals, who had been relieved by the Society during the last year; and the Auditors' Report, which shewed the highly prosperous state of the Society's Funds, was likewise read, and heard with great satisfaction.

11 *Report to members of the 1809 meeting.*

SOCIETY OF SCHOOLMASTERS.

The following is the Substance of a Letter written by a Well-wisher to the SOCIETY OF SCHOOL-
MASTERS, *which, by the desire of the Lord* BISHOP *of* CARLISLE, *who presided, was read at
their Anniversary Meeting, at the Crown and Anchor in the Strand, on the 28th December,* 1809*;
and is now printed at the unanimous request of the Company.*

26th December, 1809.

TO save myself the trouble of much writing and oral explanation, I propose to
state some of the reasons which have induced me to become an Advocate in the cause of
the Society of Schoolmasters.

A melancholy occurrence in a School, where I had two Sons, first brought me to the
knowledge of this excellent Institution. The family of the Master, consisting of six children,
was, by a singular calamity, left totally destitute of protection and support; and I was applied to, amongst other Parents, to contribute to their relief. The example was set by the
Committee of the Society of Schoolmasters, who commenced a Subscription amongst themselves; for their Institution, being then in its infancy, had not funds to afford much relief.
A sum, however, of nearly Five Hundred Pounds was soon raised, and these helpless children were snatched from poverty, and protected by the Society; and some of them have
since been placed in respectable situations.

Seeing the good effects of the Institution in this prominent case, I became immediately
a Subscriber to their Charitable Fund, and have had the good fortune to procure them many
Benefactors. It should be observed here, that they have another Fund, called the Joint Stock,
which is entirely supported by the Schoolmasters themselves, and whose families alone, are
entitled to its benefits; and this part of the Institution gives the Society a greater stability,
by ensuring the regular attendance of its Members.

But their Charitable Fund may be *beneficially applied* to any extent, being intended
for general relief; for numberless indeed are the objects of this part of the Institution, in the
persons of Decayed Schoolmasters and Ushers, and of their destitute Widows and Orphans.

12   *Thomas Hammersley's letter on behalf of the Society was originally
signed 'A Wellwisher'. Persuaded by Goodenough to acknowledge it, he
amended the signature in his own hand, 1809.*

Hammersley and the Committee may have been aware of the need for greater
and continued support but, for all this awareness, there was an assumption that all
would be well. Dr Kelly must bear some of the responsibility for this, for it was he
who almost certainly advised the Committee that they could tinker with the terms
of the Life Fund and be more generous to existing subscribers. Adoption of such a
course was an act of dangerous and, in the end, disastrous folly.

3

Dr Patrick Kelly and Growing Problems

Dr Patrick Kelly, Master of the Commercial and Mathematical Academy in Finsbury Park, was a founder member of the Society of Schoolmasters and acted as its Secretary and Treasurer for many years. He served the Society with distinction. In 1812 the Committee, in recognition of 'his long, unremitting and gratuitous services for more than 14 years', organised a subscription for him so that he might be given a suitably inscribed 'piece of plate as a lasting memorial of gratitude and esteem'.[1] A letter circulated to members suggested a donation of £1 and elicited several replies of which this is typical:

> Dear Sir,
> Your printed letter dated January 7th reached me at this place (Newbury). I am greatly pleased and I comply most readily with your proposal and accordingly enclose a one pound note, and should as readily have subscribed a much larger sum had it been required: being fully sensible of the very great service rendered by Dr Kelly to our Society and feeling individually an anxious wish to testify my respect and gratitude to him for the same.
>
> > I am Dear Sir,
> > Your very faithful Servant,
> > Geo. Scobell[2]

Kelly wielded considerable influence and both the Committee and Society came to rely on and trust his opinion – probably too much. In particular, matters concerning the Life Fund, which are minuted as 'the Committee [or sub-Committee, of which there were to be many] reported', were almost certainly those upon which Kelly had pronounced and the others had agreed. It would be surprising if Kelly did not at times see himself as indispensable – even infallible. If he did, it matters little, but what *did* matter in the years following the often reprinted Address and letter of 1809 was that his advice should have been right – and it was not.

It was not until 1817 that the Committee reported that 'there is a reason to fear, that when the zeal and ardour for the succession of new members, which exist in infant societies, shall be succeeded by that languor and indifference, which are almost inseparable from old establishments, our numbers will gradually dwindle into

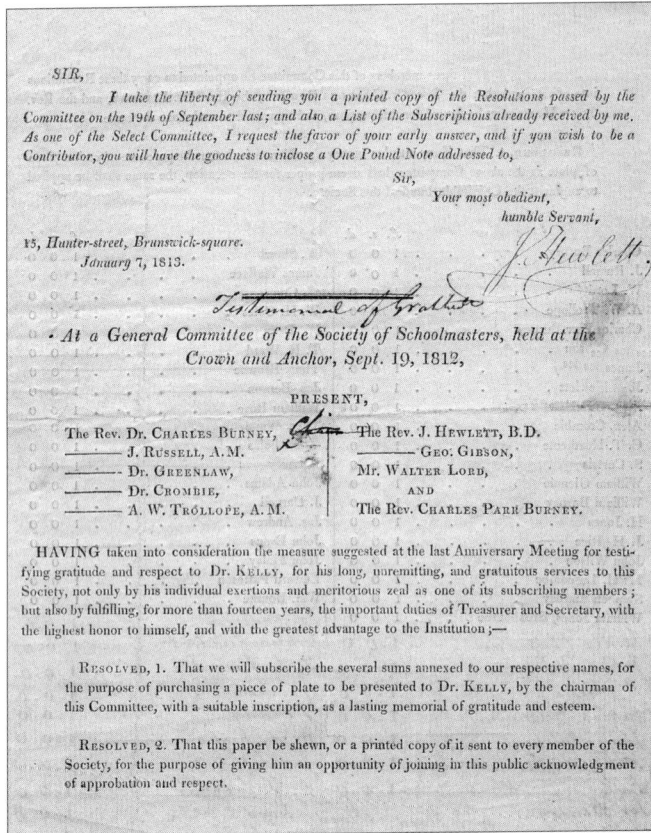

SIR,

     I take the liberty of sending you a printed copy of the Resolutions passed by the Committee on the 19th of September last; and also a List of the Subscriptions already received by me. As one of the Select Committee, I request the favor of your early answer, and if you wish to be a Contributor, you will have the goodness to inclose a One Pound Note addressed to,

                                           Sir,

                                 Your most obedient,

                                   humble Servant,

13, *Hunter-street, Brunswick-square.*
     January 7, 1813.

At a General Committee of the Society of Schoolmasters, held at the Crown and Anchor, Sept. 19, 1812,

PRESENT,

The Rev. Dr. CHARLES BURNEY,	The Rev. J. HEWLETT, B.D.
——— J. RUSSELL, A.M.	——— GEO. GIBSON,
——— Dr. GREENLAW,	Mr. WALTER LORD,
——— Dr. CROMBIE,	AND
——— A. W. TROLLOPE, A.M.	The Rev. CHARLES PARR BURNEY.

HAVING taken into consideration the measure suggested at the last Anniversary Meeting for testifying gratitude and respect to Dr. KELLY, for his long, unremitting, and gratuitous services to this Society, not only by his individual exertions and meritorious zeal as one of its subscribing members; but also by fulfilling, for more than fourteen years, the important duties of Treasurer and Secretary, with the highest honor to himself, and with the greatest advantage to the Institution;—

RESOLVED, 1. That we will subscribe the several sums annexed to our respective names, for the purpose of purchasing a piece of plate to be presented to Dr. KELLY, by the chairman of this Committee, with a suitable inscription, as a lasting memorial of gratitude and esteem.

RESOLVED, 2. That this paper be shewn, or a printed copy of it sent to every member of the Society, for the purpose of giving him an opportunity of joining in this public acknowledgment of approbation and respect.

13   *Appeal on behalf of Dr Patrick Kelly, 1812.*

insignificance.'[3] It was a comment which could easily have been made, and just as correctly, several years earlier. The signs of possible trouble had been there for some time. There had been a failure to check the ages of members and ensure that they paid the increased premiums once they had passed the age of forty. Certificates of health were not insisted on for new members – and even though no claim could be made until after the fourth subscription had been paid, a blind trust in 'healthy schoolmasters' was both a little naïve and a considerable risk. There was an increasing imbalance in ages – too many over fifty, too few under forty – which meant that premiums were out of kilter. While there had been an early rush of donations, these had not been maintained. In addition, the Life Fund had been artificially boosted by forfeitures by members who died intestate. These included the former Vice-Chairman, the Revd Dr Matthew Raine,* one-time Headmaster of Charterhouse. The dependants of such men did not qualify for benefit under the Rules of the Society. Some steps were taken to improve the administration further – a Collector of Subscriptions was appointed and fines were levied on late payers – but these made little real impact.

---

*   See Appendix II.

At this stage it was perhaps asking too much of the Committee to sort out the problems: too much was left in the hands of very busy men who held highly responsible positions elsewhere. It is also understandable that people were willing to leave much of the donkeywork to the willing Kelly, and to accept his advice and judgement. Now, at this critical moment, Kelly made a series of blunders. By 1813 it was clear that some material alterations to the Plan were necessary, but Kelly, 'encouraged by what he regarded as the increasing prosperity of the institution', recommended to the Committee that the benefits be increased by about fifteen per cent, by 'additions to some claims and a reduced period for others'.[4] He also suggested that premiums for those over forty be increased and that members took out additional shares if they wished to increase their cover – something few, in fact, did. He further proposed that new members would have to provide much greater, corroborated detail about themselves and their health. The Committee agreed, wrongly assuming that the calculations Kelly laid before them had been thoroughly and properly examined by William Morgan, Actuary of the Equitable Assurance Office. It was a major mistake. The Committee had accepted Kelly's word that Morgan was entirely happy. According to Kelly, the Society was prosperous; he continued to hold this view between 1813 and 1817. It is true that only one member resigned, the Revd Dr John Strachan, in 1814, but it is also true that in that year there were only 128 members, too few for the Society to flourish. In March 1816 the Committee received a letter from a member, W. Frend, questioning the stability of the Society, and expressing concerns about the age imbalance and the premiums charged, which he believed to be too low.

It emerged that things were not quite as Kelly had suggested. Morgan had *not* thoroughly examined Kelly's 1813 calculations and had relied too much 'on the accuracy of Dr Kelly's statement'.[5] In fact, as Kelly was later to admit, no proper calculations had been made at all. Furthermore, a suspicion held by two members of the Committee (Drs Hewlett and Crombie) that Morgan, when offering an optimistic opinion on the Life Fund, had been working from inaccurate information, was confirmed. It was not until September 1816, when he was eventually provided with accurate information, that Morgan was able to put before the Committee three plans which he hoped might, if adopted, stabilise the Fund. Morgan's view, which he repeated more than once, was that there had already been too many changes to the scheme and that payments at the top end of the scale were too high. Despite the emerging problems, Morgan's plans were not fully discussed until nine months later, in June 1817, possibly because Kelly assured everybody there was no crisis.

Morgan's first plan would have reduced the maximum claim from £300 to £250. This would have secured the Life Fund, but it was rejected, as to have done this would have broken undertakings and risked both censure and 'possible prosecution in Chancery', something which would have had 'a ruinous effect on the Society'.[6] It was also thought too complex, as was the second plan. This would have left the existing schedule in place but introduced a new scale for future members; the Committee felt that this scheme would threaten the Society with insolvency as a result of a loss of confidence; it was 'a plan so unpromising in principle, and so hazardous in its effect'.[7] The last plan was to incorporate the Society with the Equitable Assurance Office.

SOCIETY OF SCHOOLMASTERS.

—◦◦◦◦◦◦◦—

Statements and Explanations submitted to the Proprietors of the Joint Stock, *

By Dr. KELLY.

——

THE "new and important business" alluded to in the foregoing letter, is that which has been recently stated in a circular, signed by the Rev. G. GIBSON, Secretary to the Committee; but as that statement does not seem sufficiently explicit to enable the Members in general to judge of the question upon which they are called to decide, it becomes the duty of the Secretary to the Society to give further explanations. He likewise feels himself bound, as Treasurer and Trustee, to use his endeavours that the funds committed to his care be faithfully applied to the purposes for which they have been subscribed, and not risked on any experiment, much less on a speculation which he deems pregnant with danger. He considers the proposed alteration as objectionable in every point of view, even were change absolutely necessary; but he has proved, by mathematical demonstration, that no alteration on the score of instability is wanted: and in this opinion he is supported by the highest authorities on such questions—by Mr. MORGAN, Dr. HUTTON, and Mr. BAILY; who have examined and verified his calculations.

The alleged object of the proposed change is to secure the stability of the Joint Stock—and the plan is, to continue the old Society on its present footing, but to receive all future Members according to the scheme of the common assurance offices; thus, by the new table, a Member aged 32, on paying the usual premium of the Society, viz. five guineas annually, can insure his life for £200: and this sum may be claimed should he die immediately after he has paid his first subscription. By this a door is opened to fraudulent assurances, and other early losses, which are prudently guarded against in the old Society, where a Member must be of three years' standing before he is entitled to any claim, and of twenty years' before it can exceed £200. Hence, nothing can possibly be gained by such change during that long period, but great losses may be incurred; and any subsequent advantages are too remote and uncertain to be much relied upon. Nor should it be forgotten, that the old Society must guarantee all the losses, claims, and projected expenses of the new Institution; which, of course, commences without capital. This important fact is not explained in the late circular.

As there are many Members of the Society who are not well acquainted with its history, and who must be anxious to know something of the circumstances which have led to the present state of affairs, the Treasurer feels it his duty to give that information. The original plan (as begun in 1798) comprehended a life assurance scheme like the present, but the fund was augmented by voluntary subscriptions, which reduced accuracy of calculation the less necessary; and indeed, from the complicated nature of the scheme, there were no tables of temporary assurances published that could effect a perfect calculation beyond seven years, and the plan in question required them up to thirty years. Such tables, therefore, would demand a labour far disproportioned to the utility of the object. It was, however, easy to judge of the scheme, by an average comparison with the terms of the Equitable; and thus Mr. MORGAN and Dr. HUTTON were enabled, at different periods, to pronounce it a safe plan.

—————————

* This article was first annexed to the Treasurer's letter of invitation to the General Meeting (December 22, 1818). The new plan, above noticed, consisted of a table including two kinds of assurance, without any other explanation than a few sentences, calculated only to alarm and mislead. From this obscure document the Members at large were hastily called upon, at the eve of the Anniversary, to decide the fate of the Institution!!!

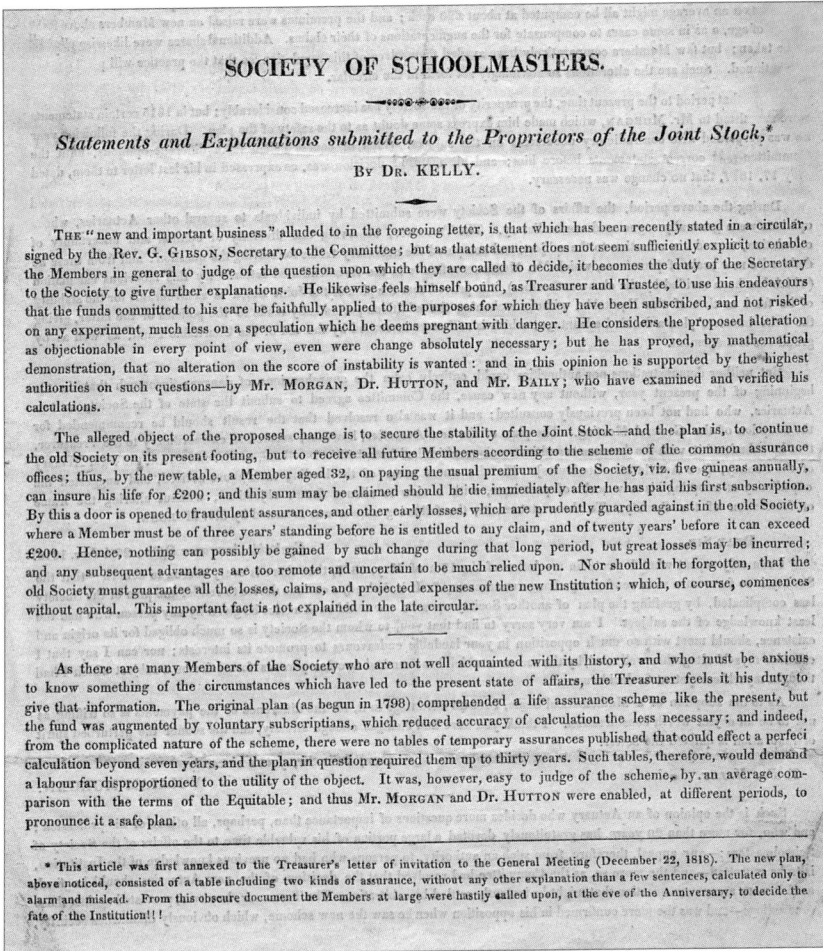

14 *Kelly defends his assessment of the Life Fund.*

Whilst this too was complex, it had the merit of allowing claims to stand as they were, giving the Society stability and thus a realistic chance of increasing the membership. The Committee was reluctant to commit itself, however, and asked Morgan to see if he could produce a scale even better suited to the circumstances of the Society. It was dithering.

Eventually the possibility of winding up the Life Fund came under discussion. In May 1817 Kelly, on behalf of the Committee, sought Morgan's view and in April 1818 the Chairman, the Revd John Russell, and Hewlett proposed such an action. The Committee was, again, reluctant to act immediately and another sub-committee was set in motion. This was to lead to division and crisis, for the sub-committee was told to put their findings 'before two [other] competent actuaries', without the knowledge of Morgan, and Kelly was asked, possibly even instructed, to provide all the documents given to Morgan, together with any written information that might be deemed necessary. The actuaries came from the Royal Exchange[8] and Atlas Assurance Offices[9] and worked independently of one another. Nevertheless, they arrived at similar conclusions, agreeing that while the Life Fund could meet the needs of existing members there were legitimate concerns about the terms to be offered to any future members, and recommended a simpler scale. In addition, both insisted on a far more rigorous enquiry into the health of any new member – the details introduced in 1813 were quite inadequate. They wanted answers to a series of questions, such as whether the candidate had 'gout, asthma, fits of any description, spitting of blood, inflammation of the lungs or liver, paralysis, dropsy or hernia'.[10] Apart from gout, for which there was an extra annual premium of 10 per cent, these conditions prevented a person from obtaining assurance.

Preferring the simpler Atlas scheme, the Committee asked for schedules to be drawn up so that they could be circulated to members together with an explanation of their concerns. By now the divisions hitherto hinted at emerged. The Atlas plan was carried in Committee by affirmation – they had once prided themselves on their unanimity. The plan was to be placed before the General Meeting for approval and Kelly, as Secretary to the Society, was asked to send out the details and the Committee's letter under his signature. He refused to do so. Thus it went out under the signature of the Secretary to the Committee, the Revd George Gibson, on 21 December 1818.

The following day Kelly sent out a circular entitled 'Statements and Explanations', in which he expressed his belief that the Committee was creating a crisis where none existed as, in his view, the Life Fund continued to flourish. His action incurred the wrath of the Committee, who now wrote again to members; Kelly had abused his office and 'converted an official document into a vehicle for his own incorrect and unauthorised statements'.[11] His paper was 'full of misrepresentations highly injurious to the character of the Committee as well as to the interests of the Society'.[12]

By now, of course, Morgan was in the picture – Kelly had sent him the findings of the Atlas and Royal Exchange Offices. Not surprisingly, Morgan dismissed their plans out of hand, commenting that he did not consider himself 'altogether well used, by the recourse which has been had to other persons for advice on a subject which he had thought himself competent to decide upon'.[13] The Committee countered that all three actuaries agreed that, unless the present plan were altered, the Society would not remain solvent. In the actuaries' view, the changes made in 1813 endangered the Society – and Kelly knew it, just as he knew that he had supplied erroneous information to Morgan. The Committee concluded that

> they found it painful to lay before the General Meeting a statement, which so deeply implicates the conduct of a member of their own body, whose services to the Society they have always appreciated and acknowledged. The Committee have been anxious to render their report as temperate as the nature of the case admitted, and much more so than the occasion might have justified.[14]

Painful it may have been, necessary it certainly was: things were coming to a head.

4

Life and Death:
The Collapse of the Life Fund

It would not be unreasonable to suppose that Dr Kelly's period in office was about to be terminated. Not a bit of it. The Annual General Meeting of December 1818 at the *Crown and Anchor* turned down the Atlas plan backed by the Committee. The Minutes recorded tersely that 'the plan recommended by the Committee in the letter was rejected'[1] and that in the elections for the 1819 Committee, Kelly was returned as Secretary and Treasurer. In its great wisdom, however, the Meeting did agree that changes to the Life Fund were essential and instructed the Committee to come up with another plan.

The Committee must have felt frustrated, if not a little peeved, after all their hard work. For W.A. Trollope of Christ's Hospital, it was all too much: 'I did not,' he wrote, 'expect to be returned a member of the Committee [in 1819], and am sorry that I am.'[2] He resigned – though he returned another year. The sub-committee which was now set up to consult with the much-put-upon Morgan about the Life Fund had no simple task, and knew it. 'It is easy enough to devise new plans which are theoretically just,' they reported, 'but what is correct in theory may be inexpedient in practice – nay, impossible to be carried out in effect.'[3] They knew only too well, of course, that Morgan had put up three plans in 1816 and might not be too keen to put up another; nor was he.

Morgan responded to their enquiry that he had considered 'the circumstances of the Society of Schoolmasters and the divisions which had unfortunately prevailed among them'. A new scale, he wrote, was urgently needed and 'the very incorrect scale published in the prospectus should be totally laid aside'[4] and his 1816 table adopted. The tone of his reply suggests that he had had enough, something confirmed in a letter written a week later. In this he said that he was pleased that the Committee now wanted to put existing and future members on the same footing but to do so was *very* complicated and

> a work of considerable labour. I am sorry to inform you that my time is so much engaged that I cannot possibly undertake the computations proposed by the Committee, and I must express a hope that this will be the last application which the Society will have to make to me on the subject.[5]

Crown & Anchor Tavern, Strand,
London, 15th March, 1821

Sir,

The Committee of the Society of Schoolmasters, being under some alarm as to the sufficiency of their Joint Stock to meet all the demands to which it is liable, from an apprehension that the risks are encreasing, or are likely to encrease, faster than the resources; & especially considering that there have been several Deaths, without any accession of new Members, within these two years, & that small hopes are entertained of any important encrease; they have appointed a Sub-committee of three Members, whose names are hereunto subscribed, to lay the state of the affairs of the Society before you, as in the annexed Abstract, & to request the favour of your answer in writing to the following queries; viz.

1st Whether, without any future accession of new Members to the Society, the Funds established will be sufficient to satisfy all the Claims to which they are liable?

2dly If an accession of new Members be requisite to enable the Society to fulfil their Engagements, to what extent will that accession be necessary?

We remain, Sir,

Your most faithf.l & obedt. Serv.ts

Jas Andrew
Walter Lord
Tom Williams

15 *The final letter from Committee seeking advice from Morgan. He refused to give it.*

I can only repeat what I have said on a former occasion, that if the Society were now to dissolve itself, & to pay every member the fair value of his interest in his assurance, the Capital of the Society will be sufficient to do it. But as the number of members is continually decreasing, & by this means becomes more & more liable to be affected by any deviation from the ordinary laws of Mortality, it is impossible to say that it is equally secure with a Society of the same kind which from the great number of its members is guarded against the danger of being seriously affected by such deviations. The Society has so often changed its plans that it has rather injured its credit, & therefore I am afraid that it is not likely to have such an accession to the number of its members as to derive any security from this source. Were the number increased to 500 or even to 400 especially on the terms lately adopted there could be no doubt of the Society's Stability. —

William Morgan

Equitable Assur Office 26 Mch 1821

16   *William Morgan of the Equitable Assurance Office shows his irritation.*

In these circumstances the Committee had little option – if they wanted to save the Life Fund – but to recommend Morgan's 1816 plan, which provided a new scale for future members and gave existing ones the option of remaining on the old or transferring to the new. The General Meeting of 1819 approved the proposal but by then the damage had been done. An increasing number of members resigned, claiming their share, and there was also an increase in the number of members who died, something over which the Society had no control. Obviously, this threatened the stability of the Fund and the Society, and an Extraordinary Committee Meeting was called in November 1820 to consider whether the 'Society should now become an Institution for Charitable purposes only … this is proposed in consequence of the great demands which are likely to be made on the Life Fund of the Society without any adequate prospect of a succession of new members.'[6] Kelly moved 'that it is expedient to divide the Life Fund among the subscribers.'[7] One might have thought that a sad, if now inevitable, decision could be reached, but, true to form, a brief

FINSBURY SQUARE, Jan. 21, 1822.

SIR,

I am directed by the Committee of the SOCIETY OF SCHOOLMASTERS to circulate the following copy of Mr. Morgan's computation of the Joint Stock, that each Proprietor may have the satisfaction to ascertain what balance is due to him, according to his number of payments.

I am, however, desired to state, that in making this calculation no adequate sum has been set apart for defraying the expenses incurred on the occasion; and therefore it is proposed that all such charges shall be paid from the Charitable Fund, and that a voluntary contribution be made, as a compensation to this Fund, from the ample dividends which are now about to be received.

Impressed with the justice and expediency of the claim, the following Members have commenced a Subscription, and the Committee are anxious that all other Members shall have an opportunity of concurring in a plan, which is the more worthy of liberal support, as the Charitable Fund has hitherto borne all the expenses of the Joint Stock, by which the dividends are so considerably augmented.

An early answer to this Circular is requested from each Member, stating the sum which he means to subscribe; and he may then expect an immediate and final settlement of his interest account, on the same general plan as the principal was transmitted.

I have the honour to be, Sir,

Your's faithfully,

P. KELLY.

SUBSCRIPTIONS RECEIVED.

Rev. C. P. Burney	The whole of his interest.	7.13.~
Mr. Fennell	ditto	10.~
Rev. Dr. Russell	ditto	19.6.~

Dr. Andrew	£15 15 0	Mr. Lord	£15 15 0
Mr. Chapman	15 15 0	Rev. Dr. Scobell	15 15 0
Mr. Haigh	5 5 0	Rev. J. Simpson	5 5 0
Rev. J. Hewlett	5 5 0	Mr. Stone	5 5 0
Mr. Hilliard	5 5 0	Mr. Wallace	5 5 0
Dr. Kelly	15 15 0	Mr. Williams	10 10 0

Each Member's different Subscriptions will be inserted in one sum in a New List, which is to be shortly published.

Copy of MR. MORGAN's Letter and Computation.

DEAR SIR,

I have at length succeeded in ascertaining the amount of the Shares of each Class of Subscribers to the Joint Stock of the Society of Schoolmasters, from which it appears that the Capital of £14,384: 16: 3 now in hand, allows of a return of each Member's Subscription, improved at compound interest of 4½ per cent, and leaves a Balance of £8: 9: 3. I congratulate you on the favourable circumstances which have enabled the Society to make such an ample distribution among its Members, and shall now take my leave of them, but not without expressing my best wishes for the success of the Charitable Fund, which I hope and trust will continue to flourish.

I remain, Dear Sir,

Your very faithful Servant,

WILLIAM MORGAN.

The Rev. JOHN HEWLETT, one of the Auditors of the Schoolmasters' Society.

17   *The Life Fund is wound up, 1822.*

Equitable Ass.ce Office 5 Feb.y 1822

My dear Sir —

I beg you would be so good as to return my best thanks to the Committee of the Society of School Masters for the very liberal manner in which they have been pleased to consider my services, and to express my regret that those services have not been more effectual in preventing the dissolution of a Society so highly honourable in respect of its members, and of the object for which it was instituted. — Accept at the same time, my dear Sir, of my warmest acknowledgments for the very kind expressions of your regard, and be assured that the civility and attention which on all occasions I have received from yourself & the other gentlemen of the Society will always be matter of sincere gratification to me. —

Believe me to be with unfeigned respect your very faithful Servant HWillMorgan

Rev. D. Russell

18   *Morgan's letter to the Committee expressing his thanks for their gift.*

stay of execution was granted in the form of a last appeal to Morgan. One can only imagine his feelings.

Morgan responded, a little irritated, on 26 March 1821, that if the Life Fund were wound up immediately, it could pay all its members fairly, but that declining numbers made it impossible to compute into the future as 'the ordinary laws of mortality'[8] on which Assurers calculated were threatened. The Society was now too small – it needed four or five hundred members to be secure – and it had changed its plans 'so often that it had injured its credit'.[9] But by this time the Committee did not need Morgan's comments; it had already held another Extraordinary Committee Meeting (10 March 1821) and reached its own conclusions and a letter was sent out calling a General Meeting for June. The Committee had decided to wind up the Life Fund and return all members their investment, together with interest, and to concentrate instead on the Charitable Fund, possibly 'establishing and supporting an Asylum or College for the reception of such aged and decayed schoolmasters, or their widows, as have made good a fair claim'.[10] This was, perhaps, a little ambitious, given the circumstances of the Charitable Fund. In June 1821 the General Meeting approved all these proposals, and the stock was sold and members notified of their share.

By December of that year, Morgan, who had this time been asked to compute the amounts due to each subscriber, had completed his work, and Kelly had written informing members of the balance due to them, together with an invitation to donate some of their profits to the Charitable Fund – something several did – as this Fund was bearing the expenses associated with the demise of the Life Fund. In all £14,384 was distributed back to members, with £6,723 having been repaid earlier. Total subscriptions to the Fund had amounted to £12,335 and so members got back their investment, together with interest of nearly seventy per cent. Kelly was keen to point out, in his covering letter, how well the two funds had done – though he made no reference to the difficulties the Charitable Fund now found itself in.

The Committee had fought a long battle to save the Life Fund, though it must share the responsibility for its collapse. Its subscriptions were probably too high, its appeal too limited; it had altered the plan too often and had moved too slowly to check early signs of weakness; it had allowed Kelly too much scope; it had failed to listen to Morgan's advice – and Morgan himself had failed to check thoroughly Kelly's figures in 1813; it had no clear idea of how to meet the crisis when it came and vacillated too long. It was a disappointing period in the Society's history and sad in other ways too. The influential Charles Burney, who had taken over from Barrow as Chairman and who had done so much to enlist powerful support, died in 1818 – the Society drew up a *Eulogium* in his memory – and Gibson, Secretary to the Committee, died in 1822 following a period of ill-health.

Despite these setbacks, the Society carried on. Annual Dinners continued come what may. In 1811, over two hundred people had sat down at the cost of 15 shillings a head, and in 1813 the Duke of Kent, having presided over the dinner, wrote from Kensington Palace that he had had an excellent time and was 'anxious to convey his appreciation of the genuine feelings of kindness he had felt and his hopes that the Society would flourish'.[11] A year later, however, the Annual Dinner made a thumping loss of £38 18s. 3d. and it is not clear how the deficit was made up; it is noticeable that in 1821 the landlord of the *Crown and Anchor*, Olley, slapped in his bill pretty quickly. There were other pleasing occurrences, such as that in 1816 when the Society began its association with a fellow schoolmaster, the Duke of Orleans,* who was in

---

* See Appendix III.

exile and teaching at Twickenham. The Minutes also reflect the calling of so many who made up the Society: dates of meetings only changed when they clashed with the Church's Kalendar. The General Meeting, for example, was moved from 22 December as this was St Thomas's Day – there would have been no such problem today as the doubting saint has been translated to 3 July!

There was one last, happier footnote to the Life Fund. In 1822 Kelly proposed that Morgan should be given a piece of plate worth 20 guineas for his services to the Society and the Life Fund in particular. Morgan's letter of pleasurable gratitude showed that at least this fence had been well mended.

5

The Charitable Fund

Charities always sought influential and wealthy patrons and the Society of School-masters was no different. During the 19th century the Committee largely consisted of the heads of great public schools, and they used their influence to attract powerful, and very necessary, support. In the early days, Burney and Hammersley were the driving forces, and their efforts saw an impressive list of donors to the Charitable Fund. Many of these were personal friends (including royalty, to whom reference will be made later): the Duke of Northumberland, Earl Spencer, Earl Chesterfield, Lords Clive, Crewe and Ferrers, the Lord Chief Justice Ellenborough, the Lord Mayor of London Alderman Heygate MP, William Wilberforce, Hannah More, Spencer Perceval (the Prime Minister murdered in the Commons by John Bellingham in 1812), Sir Robert Peel and the Whig rake, politician and playwright R.B. Sheridan all supported the charity. In addition there was a string of prominent churchmen, led by the Archbishop of Canterbury and 15 bishops, and just as long a list of schoolmasters, including the Provost of Eton, Joseph Goodall, and its Headmaster, John Keate. While support of this nature must not be underestimated, it did not bring unlimited wealth to the Society either. Many donations were one-off contributions, and so the Society could not relax its efforts to raise money if it was to continue meeting the growing number of applications for relief.

The increased numbers came from 'indigent, infirm and decayed schoolmasters', who were thought to be on the whole 'respectable', and there is no doubt that the Charitable Fund alleviated the 'distress and embarrassment' of many who had fallen on hard times. The Committee clearly got pleasure in helping 'an individual who has by their means been released from King's Bench Prison [a debtors' prison] and since settled with his wife and family in a respectable situation.'[1] Most of those helped continued to be people with large families – William Francis of Monmouth had 16 children – or who had worked well into old age, a working life of 50 years being not uncommon, and who were now blind, deaf or severely handicapped. Large families and long working lives were not, of course, peculiar to the teaching profession.

It was to meet the number of applicants that, in 1811, the amount which could be spent on cases was increased from half to two-thirds of the previous year's income. By 1813, however, applications for relief far outstripped the available income. Donations

SIR,

I have great satisfaction in being able to inform you, and the other Members of the Society of Schoolmasters, that I have lately succeeded in a cause of some interest to the Profession in general, which is, the exemption of certain School Rooms, that have been hitherto assessed, from the future payment of the Window Tax.

This important question has been thus favourably decided by His Majesty's Judges, after it had been repeatedly determined otherwise by the Commissioners of Taxes. It may be proper to explain, that I first appealed against the Assessment of my School Windows about twenty years ago, without success; and that, in consequence of subsequent Acts of Parliament, I lately renewed the appeal, but still found the Commissioners unanimous in confirming the Assessment. Being, however, convinced of the justice of my claim, I *demanded a Case*, that is, that the question should be stated for the Opinion of the Judges, which is the final appeal allowed by law. The demand was acceded to as a matter of right, and the result has been the decision of their Lordships in my favour :—but, whether the Taxes thus overpaid, which amount to above £200, will be refunded, is a question that yet remains to be determined.

I beg to annex to this Circular an Abstract of the Case as stated by the Commissioners, which may serve to shew to other Assessors the Statutes and grounds of exemption. I also add a Copy of the Judges' Opinion.

I have the honour to be,

SIR,

Your most obedient and faithful Servant,

Finsbury Square,   P. KELLY.
September 29, 1820.

19   *In 1820 Kelly won his long-running battle over the payment of Window Tax, a significant victory for many schools.*

to the Fund had varied from about £350 to £525 a year but this figure was soon to decline – in 1814 it was only £240, though this did not mean that good works ceased or were even cut back.

Besides providing financial relief, the Committee continued to defend the wider interests of the teaching profession, and in particular to protect members from the Window Tax's worst excesses. Mention has already been made of the meeting with Vansittart, and in 1820 Kelly, never too far from the action, won a case on appeal against Window Tax being applied to certain of his school's rooms. It had taken him 20 years to obtain this judgement, which was relevant to schools other than his own, and he immediately circulated members of the Society, adding the rider 'whether the taxes overpaid which amount to above £200 will be refunded, is a question that yet remains to be determined'.[2] It has a familiar ring about it.

But it was the needs of the Life Fund that had occupied the Committee between 1813 and 1818 – the Charitable Fund had been more or less neglected. In the spring

THE TIMES

THEATRE ROYAL, DRURY-LANE.
THIS EVENING, SECRETS WORTH KNOWING.
Rostrum, Mr. Elliston; April, Mr. Munden; Rose Sydney, Mad. Vestris.
After which, THE CORONATION.
To conclude with FRIGHTENED TO DEATH.

THEATRE ROYAL, COVENT-GARDEN.
THIS EVENING, THE TWO GENTLEMEN OF VERONA.
Valentine, Mr. Jones; Launce, Mr. Liston; Julia, Miss M. Tree.
After which (7th time), a new Pantomime, called
HARLEQUIN AND MOTHER BUNCH; or, The Yellow Dwarf.

THEATRE ROYAL, HAYMARKET.
ASTRONOMICAL LECTURES, on a plan not before adopted in the
metropolis, will be delivered in this Theatre during the month of
January, by Mr. GOODACRE. They will be exemplified on splendid
and original instruments, and further illustrated by numerous auxiliary diagrams. The second LECTURE will be delivered TO-MORROW
EVENING, and the gross receipts will be given to the Funds under
the direction of the Society of Schoolmasters, for the Relief of " Aged
and Decayed Schoolmasters and Ushers." During this Lecture the
Lecturer will exhibit specimens of his instruments and auxiliary
diagrams, and minutely explain his plans. He reserves to himself the
privilege of making presents to his friends, but will appropriate every
shilling of the gross receipts to the institution above mentioned.
Doors open at half past 6, the Lecture will commence 'precisely at 7,
and conclude a little before 10. Places for the boxes to be taken as
usual at the theatre. Boxes 5s., pit 3s., first gal. 2s., upper gal. 1s.—
No. 10, Panton-street, Haymarket.

ADELPHI THEATRE, Strand.
THIS EVENING, an entirely new extravaganza Burletta of Fun,
Frolic, Fashion, and Flash, in 3 acts, called TOM AND JERRY; or
Life in London. Corinthian Tom, Mr. Wrench; Jerry Hawthorn,
Mr. J. Reeve. After which an entirely new grand comic Pantomime,
called BEAUTY AND THE BEAST; or, Harlequin and the Magic
Rose. Places may be taken of Mr. Callan, at the box-office, from 10
till 4. Doors open at 6, and commence at a quarter before 7.

OLYMPIC THEATRE, Newcastle-street, Strand.
THIS EVENING, LIFE IN LONDON. Corinthian Tom, by an Ama-
teur of Fashion; Jerry, Mr. Oxberry; Logic, Mr. Vale; Snags, Mr.
Tayleure; Watchman, Mr. G. Smith; and Shuffle, Mr. Power. After
which (third time), TAG IN TRIBULATION. To conclude with an
entirely new comic Pantomime, called HARLEQUIN TATTERED
AND TORN; or, The House that Jack Built. Places may be taken
of Mr. Spring, at the Theatre.

ROYAL COBURG THEATRE.
THIS EVENING will be exhibited, the most novel, splendid, and in-
teresting object ever displayed in a British Theatre, a LOOKING-GLASS
CURTAIN, equal in extent to the ordinary drop curtain of the theatre.
A poetical Address by Miss Taylor. The performance will commence
with BEARS NOT BEASTS; or, Four Legs better than Two. After
which the splendid and terrific melo-drama, entitled THE TEMPLE
OF DEATH. To conclude with JUST ONE DOCTOR TOO MANY.
Places to be taken of Mr. Rorauer, at the theatre.

ROYALTY THEATRE, Well-street, Wellclose-square.
THIS EVENING, a new grand romantic Pantomime Spectacle, entitled NAPOLEON BUONAPARTE, General, Consul, and Emperor.
After which, Ramo Samee will go through the whole of his extraordinary Feats of Strength and Agility, concluding with his swallow-
ing a Sword two feet long. To conclude with THE CORSAIR'S SON;
or, The Fall of Otranto. Places to be taken of Mr. Nodder, at the Theatre.

☞ The publication of *The Times* commenced at 6 o'clock yesterday
morning, and finished at 8.

20 The Times, 2 February 1822. The Theatre Royal's programme included a
lecture on behalf of the Society.

of 1818, it was reported that the Fund 'was unable to give relief to *all that applied* and it was thought desirable to confine relief to schoolmasters and ushers who had contributed to the Fund of their widows and children'.[3] In the following year, a sub-committee began to look at the state of the whole Fund and the Rules relating to it. It was reported later in 1819 that the Fund's debt had increased for three years. This was because 'members of the Committee had been imperfectly acquainted with the sums received or expended by the Treasurer' and because they had failed 'to observe the Rule which limited the distribution to two-thirds of the income the preceding year'.[4] The Committee had been too generous 'out of pure compassion' for the limited means available. They had given relief to the many who had applied: 'endeavouring to accomplish too much, they have been prevented from doing enough for those who had the first claim on their liberality',[5] that is the members themselves and their 'meritorious assistants, the ushers'. Though, in practice, few seem to have suffered, the rewards had been 'too scanty as much of the Fund had been applied to other purposes'.[6] The sub-committee therefore strongly urged that future distribution should only be to these two categories, thus confirming the earlier view.

The problem had in part been caused by 'occasional teachers, masters of day schools, their ushers and families who had contrived to get the signatures of subscribers and [were] often of very questionable reputation'.[7] The Committee sensibly decided that while the Society might wish to help all who applied, to do so was incompatible with its resources and 'therefore the promiscuous application of their funds must cease'.[8] If this were done, the Committee was sure that more donations would follow, though this opinion was based more on wishful thinking than hard evidence. These measures brought a degree of control to the Charitable Fund and began 'a new era in the affairs of the Society'.[9] The Extraordinary General Meeting called to wind up the Life Fund also approved these steps, although it is fair to point out that the condition of even the Charitable Fund was far from healthy, and much careful nursing would be needed if it were to survive.

6

Royal Support

The early months of the reformed Society were spent tidying up the business associated with the Life Fund and overhauling the Charitable Fund. Procedures were tightened, the Rules rewritten and a new Public Address produced by Dr Hewlett. A new Collector of Subscriptions, John Snow, already Collector for another charity, the Literary Fund, was appointed – and Kelly was told to find out the best way to promote the Society and raise funds. As a result it became much more difficult to obtain relief – of 16 petitions considered in September 1822, eight were rejected for being unsigned or invalid or because the applicant had already received relief during the year. An application from John Waterman of Bromley was referred back to his master, Dean, whose reply failed to convince the Committee. In 1823 a letter 'as short as possible' was sent 'to all gentlemen of the profession'[1] stating the objects of the Charitable Fund and how they might support it, either through annual subscription or by donations.

An air of confidence began to return to the Society. The new Bishop of Chester, C.J. Blomfield, a man of high ambition who would later be translated to London, willingly became President; Olley of the *Crown and Anchor* was paid off and the Society moved to new premises, those of the Literary Society Fund in Lincoln's Inn Fields; a tin box was bought for £1 14s. 6d. 'for the preservation of the Society's papers,'[2] something it still does. Particular help was given where it was necessary, as in the case of Henry Morini who received £3 'to procure his release from the Debtors Prison,'[3] and refused if there were good grounds – James Woodcock 'was not found worthy of receiving any assistance.'[4] By 1824 the Society was on a more even financial keel, but when Burney, who had since 1822 occupied the office of Chairman which his father had once held, again circulated the professions and society in general for patronage and subscriptions, he pointed out that, for all its good intentions, the Society was not well-known – a point that had been made before and would be again. Burney knew just how important it was to have influential backers and patrons who were not only wealthy, but generous. As the Society had discovered earlier, the royal presence at the Annual Dinner boosted both attendance and funds, but the Society needed to cultivate this further.

It was the older Burney who had won this royal support for the Society, persuading the Duke of Cambridge, son of George III, to be the Patron, and his royal brothers, the

SOCIETY OF SCHOOLMASTERS

Instituted for the Relief of Distressed Schoolmasters and Ushers, and of their Widows and Orphans.

PATRON.

His Royal Highness PRINCE ADOLPHUS FREDERIC, DUKE OF CAMBRIDGE.

PRESIDENTS.

The Right Rev. GEORGE ISAAC HUNTINGFORD, D.D. & F.R.S. Lord Bishop of Hereford.
The Right Rev. SAMUEL GOODENOUGH, D.C.L. F.R.A. & L.S. Lord Bishop of Carlisle.

HONORARY PRESIDENTS.

The Right Hon. & Right Rev. WILLIAM HOWLEY, D.D. F.R.S. & F.A.S. Lord Bishop of London.
The Right Rev. THOMAS BURGESS, D.D. & F.R.S. Lord Bishop of St. David's.

VICE-PRESIDENTS.

The Reverend SAMUEL PARR, D.C.L. Prebendary of St. Paul's.
The Reverend JOSEPH GOODALL, D.D. Provost of Eton, & Canon of Windsor.
The Reverend WILLIAM BARROW, D.C.L. & F.A.S. Prebendary of Southwell.
The Very Reverend GERARD ANDREWES, D.D. Dean of Canterbury.

Benefactors entitled to act as Members of the Committee without Election

Andrew, James, D.C.L. Woodford, Essex	Goodenough, Rev. Edmund, D.D. Westminster	Peel, Right Hon. Robert, M.P. *Secretary of State*
Andrews, Rev. G. D.D. Dean of Canterbury, V.P.	Hereford, Lord Bishop of, PRESIDENT	Pinckney, Rev. John, D.D. East Sheen
Barbar, Robert, Esq. Charter-house	Hewlett, Rev. John, B.D. Brunswick-square	Plimley, Rev. Henry, Cuckfield
Barrow, Rev. W. D.C.L. Southwell, Nottingham-	Hooker, Rev. John, D.D. Rottingdean	Russell, Rev. John, D.D. Charter-house
shire, V.P.	Horne, Rev. T. Chiswick	Scobell, Rev. George, D.D. Henley
Bellamy, Rev. J. W. Merchant Tailors' School	Hutton, John, Esq. Richmond, Yorkshire	Simpson, J. Esq. Worcester
Burney, Charles, Esq. Greenwich	Irvine, Rev. Andrew, B.D. Charter-house	Sleath, Rev. John. D.D. St. Paul's School
Burney, Rev. Charles Parr, D.D. ditto	Keate, Rev. J. D.D. Eton	Spencer, Rt. Hon. Earl, St. James's-place
Burney, Richard, Esq. Christ's-Coll. Cambridge	Kelly, P. LL.D. Finsbury-square	SUSSEX, H.R.H. the DUKE of
Butler, Rev. George, D.D. Harrow	Lancaster, Rev. Mr. Wimbledon	Thomson, Rev. ——, D.D. Exeter
Butler, Rev. Samuel, D.D. Shrewsbury	Law, Messrs. Ave Maria-lane	Trollope, Rev. W. A. D.D. Christ's-hospital
CAMBRIDGE, H.R.H. the DUKE of, PATRON	London, Lord Bishop of, HON. PRES.	Turner, Rev. Lewis, Weowil-brook, Cardiganshire
Carlisle, Lord Bishop of. PRESIDENT	Longman, Messrs. Paternoster-row	Valpy, Rev. Richard, D.D. Reading
Chapman, James, Esq. Wandsworth-lane, Putney	Lord, Walter, Esq. Tooting	Warner, Simeon, Esq. Blackheath
Chester, Lord Bishop of	Nicholas, Rev. George, D.C.L. Ealing	Watkinson, Rev. Robert, B.D. Charter-house
Edwards, Rev. Richard, late of St. Paul's School.	ORLEANS, H.R.H. the DUKE of	Watson, Joshua, Esq. Clapton
Exeter, Lord Bishop of	Ouiseau, J. Esq.	Whittaker, Messrs. Ave Maria-lane
Cabell, Rev. H. D. D.D. late of Winchester	Parr, Rev. Samuel, D.C.L. Hatton, V.P.	Williams, Rev. David, D.C.L. Winchester
Glennie, William, LL.D. Dulwich	Payne, Thomas, Esq. Pall-mall	Wooll, Rev. John, D.D. Rugby.
Goodall, Rev. Jos. D.D. Provost of Eton, V.P.	Pearson, Rev. J. D.D. East Sheen	

ACTING COMMITTEE for 1824.

Burney, Rev. C. P. D.D. *Chairman*	Hewlett, Rev. J. *Auditor*	Russell, Rev. J. D.D. *Treasurer*
Carmalt, Rev. W.	Hilliard, R. Esq.	Scobell, Rev. J. D.D.
Chapman, James, Esq. *Secretary*	Kelly, P. LL.D.	Sleath, Rev, J. D.D. *Auditor*
Chapman, Rev. T.	Lord, Walter, Esq. *Auditor*	Stone, G. Esq.
Dallin, Rev. Robert	Morris, Rev. J. D.D.	Trollope, Rev. W. A. D.D.
Drury, Rev. W.		

TRUSTEES OF THE FUND.

Barrow, Rev. W. D.C.L.	Kelly, P. LL.D.	Burney, Rev. C. P. D.D.

The LITERARY FUND SOCIETY having, with great kindness and liberality, offered the use of their Chambers in Lincoln's-Inn-Fields to the Schoolmasters' Society, the Committee will meet at those Chambers on the First Saturday in February, April, October, and December, to receive applications for Relief.

Subscribers are requested to be very particular in stating *how long* they have known the parties whose Petitions they counter-sign; in what School they were employed; what has been their character; and what are their present means of support.

Charter House, Dec. 18, 1824.

J. RUSSELL,
Treasurer of the Society.

21 *The Society promoted itself in 1824.*

Dukes of Kent and Sussex, to make donations. Like the Prince Regent, the brothers were held in almost universal contempt and were ridiculed by the pen of Thackeray and in the caricatures of Rowlandson and Gillray. The Duke of Wellington had no time for them: 'they are the damnedest millstone about the necks of any government that can be imagined. They have insulted – personally insulted – two thirds of the gentlemen of England.' Where this leaves the gentlemen of the Society is uncertain! All the brothers except Cambridge, who spent most of his time in Hanover, spent money with gay abandon and littered the land with illegitimate offspring. Kent's insistence on the severest military discipline led to a mutiny in Gibraltar; pot-bellied,

22 *The ambitious and able Bishop of London, Charles James Blomfield, who worked effectively on behalf of the Society.*

with dyed receding hair, he lived with Madame St Laurent, a French-Canadian, for 27 years before passing her over for Victoire, Princess of Leiningen, and possibly fathering Victoria – still an open question. Sussex had a warm heart but married foolishly and was hugely extravagant. Cambridge was a strange, often mean, man 'with a loud, bellowing voice' and he immediately 'answered any rhetorical questions the parson mistakenly inserted into his sermon … Card sharpers and crooks, the riff-raff of society were to be found at [the brothers'] table.' 'Self-indulgent vulgarity'[5] it may have been, but it brought the Society some benefits. In 1825 George IV, 'Prinny' and the eldest of the brothers, made a donation of 100 guineas, and the following year converted this into an annual subscription of 50 guineas, a practice William IV continued on George's death in 1830. Queen Victoria also followed suit, but only for a time. Any optimism was to be short-lived, however.

One problem for the Society had always been how to maintain momentum once established, and by 1849 it was clear that the Society was again ticking over and struggling, short of members, funds and ideas. The confidence of 25 years earlier had taken a knock and was about to take another. In that year George Edward Anson, Keeper of Her Majesty's Privy Purse, wrote from Balmoral forwarding a *donation* of 20 guineas from the Queen to the Society, not the 50 guineas *subscription* that had been expected. Anson wrote, 'Her Majesty is desirous of doing the greatest good

23   *Queen Victoria's withdrawal of financial support was to put the Society into some disarray.*

she can to Charities' and not always 'by continuing annual subscriptions to the same charities – and it would appear from a report which you have forwarded to me, that Her Majesty's continued subscription to this Charity, has not been productive of that public good which it ought to have been, supposing that more energy had been infused into its management.'[6] She had contributed 50 guineas in the past but

> the whole of the rest of the donations and subscriptions for the past year amount only to £139.6.0. This does not prove a wholesome state of management, if the Charity is a good one on public grounds. The 20 guineas I enclose a check [*sic*] for I call a Donation, and its continuance will depend upon the exertions which are made to maintain and uphold the Charity.[7]

Russell, as Treasurer, replied at length, thanking the Queen for her donation and assuring Anson that the Committee was very keen to 'merit the continued support of a sovereign who dispenses charity with so much equity and discrimination.'[8] He pointed out that when her father, the Duke of Kent, presided over the Society's public dinners, 'those who were not schoolmasters gladly came and gave liberally at his bidding. Since his time the public dinners have discontinued'[9] as people no longer came to see or be seen. He further emphasised the poverty of most schoolmasters, and suggested that Anson had apparently missed a recent bequest of £1,000 to relieve distress and he hoped that this would be taken into account in the future.

In the light of this experience, the Society wheeled out its big guns for the General Meeting of 1850: the Archbishop of Canterbury, J.B. Sumner, took the Chair as President, and alongside him were the Bishops of London (Blomfield) and St Asaph (T.V. Short). The Society emphasised how it had sought to widen its appeal and engender greater support. And so Russell tried again, writing to the new Keeper, the Honourable Colonel C.B. Phipps, and adding, perhaps unwisely, that sadly the Society had lost its Patron and benefactor of 38 years' service, the Duke of Cambridge, and would the Prince Albert care to replace him, as they were 'soliciting the countenance and protection of one who is distinguished no less for his zeal in behalf of literature and science than for his illustrious station.'[10]

Phipps did not take long to reply.

> I am commanded to state to you in reply that Her Majesty observes that in the List of Donations and Subscriptions Her Majesty's name is still inserted as a subscriber of £52.10.0 whereas that subscription was withdrawn last year, and a donation of £21 substituted. This somewhat detracts from the value of the [last] Report. It also appears that the amount of subscriptions for the last year amount to only £117 and that (excluding schoolmasters) there are not annual subscribers above about £10. These facts render it clear to Her Majesty that the Institution as at present regulated, either does not answer the requirements of the public, or it does not excite its sympathies, and I have therefore received no commands from Her Majesty to make any donation this year to the Society. Should any new connection with … the Council of Education, or any Provident Society of Schoolmasters, impart new vitality to this project for the support of decayed schoolmasters, Her Majesty would always be ready to take into her gracious consideration any plan that might prove effective in affording aid to this highly deserving class of Her Majesty's subjects.[11]

Sufficiently chastened, the Society licked its wounds and returned to its normal work. In an attempt to win subscribers it strengthened and extended the Local Representatives, but there is no denying that, for the next two years or so, the Society rather limped along: one can almost feel the despondency.

The Hanoverians were not the only royal patrons of the Society. It also enjoyed the support of Louis Philippe, King of the French from 1830-48. As Duc d'Orleans Louis Philippe, a descendant of Louis XIII, had been in exile in England in 1816. During this time Kelly had been in correspondence with him, seeking to enlist his support, for he had been a teacher for eight months during his exile – a time he described as one of 'severe distress and persecution.'[12] D'Orleans was indeed very interested in

SCHOOLMASTERS.—At the Anniversary Dinner on Friday, the Duke of SUSSEX, who presided, mentioned that the Duke of ORLEANS, in answer to an invitation to attend the meeting, had sent 10 guineas, stating, that he had himself once been a schoolmaster, and had in the time of his adversity relied for his support on his talents and acquirements. The health of the Duke of ORLEANS was then drank, on the proposition of the Duke of SUSSEX, as " The Royal Schoolmaster," with great delight.

We are happy to state, that Mr. PLATT is recovering rapidly from the effect of his wound. It has been determined not to cut for the ball. If the ball retain its spherical form, it may work out of some other part of the body, without affecting the health of the patient.

A subscription has been entered into at Glasgow for the relief of the poor. The sum subscribed by the first ten on the list amounted to not less than 1,600*l.*

A reward of 200 guineas is offered in Saturday's *Gazette* for the discovery of the person or persons who, in the night of the 16th instant, set fire to a wheat-stack belonging to Mr. W. Downing, of Denton, Lincolnshire, with the promise of a free pardon to any accomplice making such discovery.

On Friday evening the house of Mr. Munroe, No. 8, Gun-lane, Limehouse, was broken open during the absence of the family, by means of a skeleton key, and robbed of plate and wearing apparel to a considerable amount.

SHOCKING MURDER.—We are concerned to record one of the most wanton murders that has for a long time come to our knowledge. A man, named Aickens, employed as bailiff to drive the cattle of a respectable farmer, of the name of Keeshan, on the lands of Carrick, near Roscrea, in the county of Tipperary, on Friday morning last, for non-payment of rent, when his son, Mr. Daniel Keeshan, very quietly requested to see the authority under which he acted: the fellow replied, " You shall soon see that," and, pulling a pistol from his pocket, shot the unfortunate young man through the heart! This dreadful affair is the more to be regretted, as the deceased was a young man of the most exemplary conduct and inoffensive manners. He had served in the British army as a surgeon, having graduated in the Royal College of Surgeons in this city, and had some time since retired to his father's place on half-pay. Aickens, we are happy to hear, has been apprehended, and committed to the gaol of Roscrea.—*Dublin paper.*

24 The Times, 23 December 1816. *Annual Dinner at which the Duke of Sussex proposes the health of the Duke of Orleans.*

the Society, and he hoped that the Society would 'permit him to tender his mite as a "fellow schoolmaster"'. He had lived in Twickenham before returning to France to become the centre of middle-class opposition to the restored monarchy, and when Charles X fell in 1830, he was chosen as King, beginning a regime known as the July Monarchy. He reigned until 1848, 'the year of revolutions', when he was forced to flee again to England, having refused to consider electoral reforms.

25   *John Bird Sumner, Archbishop of Canterbury and President 1848-62.*

In 1844 Russell, the Treasurer and former Headmaster of Charterhouse, had written to the King reminding him of his contribution in 1816 and of his attendance at a Dinner, which had been held that year to celebrate the Duke of Kent's birthday, and at which he had met both Kelly and Russell, who was at that stage Chairman. The letter was sent to Francois Guizot, once a Professor of History in Paris, who had formed the Primary Education Law of 1835 and was now Foreign Minister before his brief time as Prime Minister (1847-8). Guizot, having refused to make any political concessions, was also forced into exile in England where, despite a reputation for clumsy dealings with the British, he formed a close friendship with Sir John Boileau of Ketteringham Hall in Norfolk.[13] Russell's letter worked – the King sent two further donations.* Powerful support like this was important in promoting the Society, especially in the early years.

But the Society needed more than royal support, helpful though these subscriptions and donations were. When they ceased, in the 1840s, the Society was pretty moribund: membership and funds had been in decline from the 1830s and the Committee, several of whom had served faithfully for a long time, had run out of ideas. Change was needed to inject new life. It came, but not immediately.

By way of comparison the Governesses' Benevolent Institution (GBI) had been formed as the Governesses' Mutual Assurance Society in 1829 to help those governesses who were suffering from hardship, illness or old age. By 1838, the year

---

*   See Royal Correspondence, Appendix III.

Council will remedy this.—*Hertford Reformer.*
SCHOOLMASTERS' SOCIETY.—(From a Correspondent.)
—The annual general meeting of the Society of Schoolmasters was held on Saturday, the 17th instant, at the
chambers of the Literary Fund Society, in Lincoln's-inn-
fields. At this meeting the usual routine business was
gone through, and the officers for the ensuing year were se-
lected. A committee meeting took place previously, at which
relief was granted to the most deserving objects of the charity,
in various sums, amounting to nearly 100*l*. The members of
the committee and their friends afterwards dined together at
the Freemasons' Tavern. In the course of the evening, after
the usual toasts, much regret was expressed, as on previous
occasions, that the existence and merits of this society appear
to be still too little known to the profession at large. Although several new subscribers joined it at this anniversary,
they were yet much fewer than were expected. It should be
stated for the information of schoolmasters and others engaged in tuition, that the society is exclusively a charitable
society, for the relief of distressed masters and ushers, and of
their widows and children ; that it is honoured with the highest patronage, His Majesty being an annual subscriber of 50*l*. ;
that his Grace the Archbishop of Canterbury is the President ; that several of the bench of bishops, and of late distinguished heads of public schools, who have retired from
the profession, are among the vice-presidents ; and that the
present list of subscribers contains the names of most of the
head masters of the principal public schools. But from among
private schoolmasters, and the masters of the new proprietary
schools, the number of contributors is comparatively very
small. The regret felt on this account is not unattended by
a hope that this useful society will be sought out and supported, as it deserves to be, when its claims are duly considered, by the affluent and humane. They who derive their
portion of the blessings of this life, under Providence, chiefly,
if not wholly, from the well-earned reward of their labours in
teaching, will surely not hesitate to embrace the opportunity
afforded them by this society of alleviating the distresses of
their less successful brethren in their hour of need.

26   The Times, *21 December 1836. The report of the
Committee Dinner laments declining numbers.*

of the People's Charter, it had folded. Attempts were made in 1841 and 1843 to refloat it as the Governesses' Benevolent Fund and the Governesses' Provident Fund and in 1843 the Revd David Laing was appointed as Honorary Secretary. Laing was to be the founder of the GBI; a Scotsman of remarkable vision and energy, for whom no task was too great, he was 'above all human'.[14] He was also the incumbent of Holy Trinity, St Pancras, a parish with a population of 9,000 but without a church. Laing raised the money to build one and he increased his congregation from 23 to 1,500 – all within three years. As Founder of GBI he started with £100 in the bank and very few subscribers. Within a year there were 600 names on the subscription list and, by the time he died in 1860, this number had increased to 6,000. When '47 noblemen and gentlemen'[15] sat down to dinner at the *London Tavern* to hear Dickens speak in 1844, Laing had attracted five royal patrons. The Queen gave her name to the Queen's College, which was founded in 1847 to train governesses, with the Christian Socialist F.D. Maurice as its first Principal. Laing had also opened a house in Harley Street where governesses could stay.

While it would be quite wrong to compare SOS with GBI too closely, it is easy to discern some parallels. What does become clear is that GBI was able to develop and broaden its appeal and influence in a way that SOS was, or rather did, not. By 1890 GBI had over £558,000 invested in its Provident Department, 288 women were receiving annuities, and temporary grants were made to over 22,000 applicants, totalling more than £59,000. In the same year, SOS helped 38 people at a cost of £458. Yet bald figures, of course, only tell a little of the story.*

---

*   There were other clergymen who did similar things in the East End of London to Laing: Canon Samuel Barnett, curate at Bethnal Green and then vicar of St Jude's, Whitechapel, and the Revd Charles Lowder and his curate the Revd L.S. Wainwright, at St Peter's, London Docks, were among them.

7

A Remarkable Group of Men

The main support for the Society came not from the often erratic help of the famous but the continued backing of the Church and the teaching profession itself. Not surprisingly these are intertwined, for most schoolmasters, certainly during the first half of the 19th century, were clerics. Many of them, following a short period teaching at their university as Fellows, went on to preferment in the Church or Headships of great schools or both. Many such men served the Society actively over long periods and promotion did not stop their work for it. Interestingly, individuals who got a poor or mixed press in their professional lives often showed a very different side in their work for the Society, developing its role and giving it generous financial support. The Society has been well served throughout its history by its devoted Committees and Officers.

In 1797 the great public schools may have attracted prestige, but their curriculum was strictly classical – 'modern' subjects like science were anathema – and few would suggest that these schools were as efficient, humane or disciplined as they were to become. A great deal depended on the headmaster, who wielded considerable power. For a long time the alternative to the public schools had been the grammar and privately run schools, but by the reign of Victoria these had been in decline for many years – at Whitgift's Hospital, Croydon, a master found no pupils when he arrived and left none when he died 30 years later! The grammar schools, many of which had been founded in the 16th and 17th centuries, came nowhere near meeting the demands of the 19th century. Their endowments did not allow them to employ good staff – the head of a major public school might earn £1,000 a year, and assistant masters would be poached at good salaries from their Fellowships at Oxford and Cambridge to teach in such schools. Nor did the endowments allow them to improve tired and scruffy buildings – the grammar school at Lancaster was described as 'ugly without and dirty within'.

That change would have to come was evident from the demands of the rising middle class which were fuelled by the industrial, agricultural and transport revolutions. Parents demanded a more practical education, vocationally guided, with good handwriting and arithmetic being taught and not classics and sermons. In the second half of the century, schools such as Marlborough (founded in 1843), Wellington

27 *Dr John Sleath, High Master of St Paul's School, prominent Committee member and one of the great classicists of his day.*

28 *A rare image of Dr John Keate, drawn by a young Etonian … while the Headmaster was teaching.*

(1859) and Lancing (1848) came to meet the needs of the middle classes and to follow Thring's lead at Uppingham by introducing more games, but for the first part of the century the gentry continued to be educated at the old public schools.

It would be quite wrong to expect the Society of Schoolmasters to do other than reflect the society in which they lived and, broadly, there are three inter-linked periods within the 19th century which represent these changes. Initially, the Society was dominated by men of the classical tradition, then by those who had come under the influence of Arnold and Godliness and Good Learning, and lastly by those who added a touch of Muscular Christianity to what had gone before.

At the outset, the membership and the Committee represented the great public schools and the classical tradition embodied by men like the Revd Dr John Sleath, High Master of St Paul's School and one of the greatest defenders of the classical curriculum, and Dr Edward Maltby, Bishop of Chichester and then of Durham. Maltby, who examined regularly at St Paul's, would not have been out of place in Trollope; he was hated by the Tories, as an ancient Whig who lived 'remote from affairs and from men.'[1] Both men worked on behalf of, and gave to, the Society. A Vice-President and benefactor was the Revd Dr John Keate, Headmaster of Eton between 1809 and 1834. Keate's reputation as a brutal flogger may have been merited, but there was more to Keate than this; he tried to get the best out of boys in the classroom and, as has been pointed out by many, he did realise that between childhood and manhood there was a creature called a boy, something Thomas Arnold did not understand.[2] Interestingly, Sleath's St Paul's produced James Prince Lee and Keate's Eton produced Edward Thring and these two came to represent the second and third periods.

During the early period the President had been a Bishop (of Gloucester and Hereford), but from 1832 until 1903 the Society enjoyed the support of the Archbishops of Canterbury. In 1832 this was William Howley, formerly Bishop of London and once Regius Professor of Divinity at Oxford. A small man, Howley was no fool and was tough enough to have knocked Sydney Smith down with a chessboard when at Winchester but, though much loved, he was perceived as weak and was certainly no orator – he found it difficult to select the right word and 'his speeches sounded like those of an imbecile.'[3] The evangelical Sumner's sermons were considered sane, even eloquent, when compared with those of Howley.[4] For all this, he was a respected and hard-working President, as were his successors, J.B. Sumner, C.T. Longley, A.C. Tait, E.W. Benson and F. Temple. It was Howley who, together with Blomfield, Bishop of London, engineered a donation to the Society of £100 from the Trustees of the Cholmondely Fund in 1837. Support also arrived from one of Maltby's predecessors at Durham, Dr Shute Barrington (1791-1862), but these men, like most members of the Society, were wealthy, intelligent, traditional and influential enjoyers of the good things in life, such as the dinners at the *Crown and Anchor*. Perhaps the wig encapsulates the sort of men they were: Shute Barrington may have been the first bishop to discard the wig, though it is more likely to have been Blomfield, and by 1832 most bishops had given them up. Not, however, Howley, who continued to wear his until his death in 1848, and Sumner wore one in church until he died in 1862.[5]

It might be thought that such men would be totally out of touch with changing society, but this is not the case. Dr Patrick Kelly ran a successful school which provided the middle classes with the sort of vocational training they increasingly wanted for their children. The Committee also shared a common wish, increasingly obvious after the collapse of the Life Fund, to help those of the profession who were in need. Though they realised, of course, that aid could not be offered to

29 *A letter to* The Times *dated 1 January 1828 critical of caning in schools hints that the Society is less so.*

TO THE EDITOR OF THE TIMES.

Sir,—The letter of "A Titled Candidate for Holy Orders," cannot be read without interest ; and whatever he may think of my mistakes, I can do justice to the purity of his motives, and commiserate the ungrateful return which he has experienced. He speaks of having delivered two sermons in the school-room, and I cannot but wish he had said, read, because there may arise a suspicion that they were extemporaneous effusions ; and it can hardly be imagined, from the onerous nature of his occupation, that he could even compose, much less commit to memory, any thing like two well-digested discourses every week ; besides, as he possesses in an eminent degree what I by no means think a mean acquirement, his judgment and taste would be both evinced by reading from the best theological writers, those sermons which he considered most adapted to the understandings of his auditors. As regards school assistants, all my prejudices are on their side, for I never had the least cause to complain of their conduct ; on the contrary, I owe them a debt of gratitude: but as to the masters, I confess I can make no such declaration, and perhaps I shall be suspected of a wish to pay off old scores, when I say that I should not be sorry to see a day of retribution, when all the race, from the natty crop to the large bush wig, who have exercised and delighted in that elegant kind of correction, should have one good flogging from their pupils, and that then the practice should be for ever abolished, and, in the words so often used to boys, a new leaf be turned over. This application à posteriori, I believe, would have more effect than a thousand arguments. Had I birch coppice, I would cheerfully cut it down for the purpose ; and I will most readily subscribe all the twigs and scions of my favourite plantations, as substitutes, which I have known applied with admirable skill. If the boys should want assistance, I trust the race of Bowlings is not extinct. I have been witness to the greatest tyranny and the most disgusting levity, in the infliction of a punishment that for its indecency should be banished, at least from beyond the precincts of the nursery, if even admitted there. I have seen an urchin of seven years old undergoing such chastisement for not repeating a collect by heart, though he pleaded very truly to his master that he had made a mistake, and had learned more than half of a wrong one, and would say the greater part of that which was the right, and which he had commenced when he discovered his error. Though it was his first offence, and he was the best arithmetician of his age in the school, he could not avert the rod by showing that two halves were equal to a whole, and he was taught experimentally the meaning of Black Monday. The sense of indignity and disgrace stuck to the boy, and he convinced the master, by ever after sedulously shunning his presence, that he retained a strong sense of what he considered a harsh and severe infliction.

At Eton and other public schools, as well as private seminaries, such an odious practice is persisted in, even to the verge of manhood. I can well believe that there are natures so constituted, that no disgrace is sensibly felt, and that the bearing a sharp flogging, instead of learning a long lesson, is considered no bad compounding. With such obtuseness they grow up, and think it a trifle for others to submit to what they thought so little of themselves. They have experienced tyranny, and they become tyrants.

Would you seek amongst those who have been hardened by the repetitions of such things for those qualities which adorn and do honour to human nature ? I should as soon select the man who had been tied up to the halberds, for any peculiar trust, or for the performance of any difficult or heroic exploit. If I made such a choice, it would be opposed to the experience of officers, who declare, that when a man has undergone the disgrace of stripping, he is no longer worth any thing as a soldier. Dr. Johnson is quoted as a great authority, and yet I think his observation is rather a sarcasm on the custom, than a defence ; but it must be recollected he had been a pedagogue. Should you wish to learn whether a certain occupation tended to degrade the human mind, would you ask the person who was so employed ? For instance, would you ask the hangman, or public executioner, whether his morals were deteriorated by his profession ? You may just as well ask schoolmasters the effect of their conduct, though let it not be imagined I mean any comparison between them and the outcasts of society to whom I have alluded. Palliatives, in speaking of this matter, I am sure will have no effect ; a total renunciation is required of what has been too long permitted ; and our posterity, I have no doubt, will wonder how such a practice should have ever been introduced. The moment it is abolished, it will be acknowledged to be execrable.

Should the authority of Solomon be quoted, I will answer that I believe he never intended that he should be quoted, as an excuse, for applying such a stimulant, and in such a way, to youths who have any sense of shame.

I will, however, conclude ; and should I be threatened, that the Society of Schoolmasters have " a rod in pickle for me," it will not be the first time I have heard the threat.

If I ever address you again, it will be on some other subject.   FIAT JUSTITIA.

30   *Thomas Arnold, Headmaster of Rugby School 1828-42, whose influence on his staff and pupils was to spread throughout the educational world and through the Society.*

all, they were well aware of the lack of pensions and health services and the fact that too many, short of pupils and income, were living on hope. But, for all these good intentions, the 1830s and '40s can hardly be described as the most exciting in the Society's history.

That the Society did evolve at all was in part due to the indirect influence of Arnold of Rugby, many of whose protégés, either as pupils or staff, came to sit on the Committee, replacing those who had served for so long. They brought with them a somewhat different approach. Arnold had succeeded Dr John Wooll[*] in 1828; Wooll had been a respected and efficient Head, but Rugby remained a school where the 'boys could be regarded as the excrescences of pond life.'[6] Arnold's work and influence

---

*   Wooll, Headmaster from 1808-28, had presided over the acquisition of new school buildings at a cost of £46,000. The publicity resulted in an intake of over 100, the largest of any school in England. Numbers then fell way until Arnold's time.

31 *Several prominent churchmen and schoolmasters were influenced by Arnold and continued his traditions. These included C.J. Vaughan, Head-master of Harrow School.*

32 *Christopher Wordsworth, also Head of Harrow.*

33 *G.H. Moberley, Head-master of Winchester College.*

has been well documented, not least by one of his former pupils, A.P. Stanley,[*] Dean of Westminster and a member of the Society, and there is little to be gained from rehearsing information which can be gained easily elsewhere. Two points should, however, be emphasised in relation to the Society of Schoolmasters, of which Arnold was himself a member from 1830, not especially surprising in view of the fact that so many were, including two-thirds of the bench of bishops. Firstly, Arnold, who was Chaplain as well as Headmaster, saw the value of the sermon and of preaching to boys regularly – unlike at Eton, where sermons were so ineffably boring that the Head, Dr Balston, another member of the Society, was criticised on this score by Lord Clarendon when he appeared before the Public Schools Inquiry Commission[†] in 1862. Arnold's preaching left a deep impression on his pupils, inspiring many to follow his example. One such was C.J. Vaughan,[‡] Headmaster of Harrow (1844-59), Dean of Llandaff and Master of the Temple Church, who was able and willing to carry on the Arnoldian system. Secondly, Arnold appointed to his staff like-minded, public-spirited reformers and they, along with his pupils, became his disciples and, like Vaughan, saw it as their mission to train Christian gentlemen to organise efficiently, to be men of character, and to have a *sense of social duty*. It was such men who were to run the Society during the mid-century.

James Prince Lee was one of those appointed by Arnold to Rugby. Lee had been a boy at St Paul's, where both Sleath and Maltby had noted his quality. He had

---

[*] Stanley was the real-life model for Arthur in *Tom Brown's Schooldays*. He was the son of a Bishop of Norwich with a family history going back before Flodden. In 1864 he counted amongst his relatives the Post Master General (Earl of Elgin), the Foreign Secretary and next Prime Minister (Russell) and the next Foreign Secretary (Clarendon).

[†] Set up in 1861 to look into the condition of the nine great public schools, it reported in 1864.

[‡] Vaughan was destined for high office before he left Harrow suddenly; his homosexuality remained secret until 1964. Vaughan had been a pupil at Rugby and had married Stanley's sister in 1850.

34 *T.W. Jex Blake, Head of Cheltenham and Rugby.*

35 *Edward White Benson, the first Headmaster of Wellington College and later Archbishop of Canterbury, was a protégé of James Prince Lee – who had also been inspired by Arnold.*

gone on to be one of the finest classical minds of his day at Cambridge before being appointed to Rugby in 1830, where he spent eight years being hugely influenced by Arnold, even though he did not always agree with him. Lee was the first Cambridge man to be appointed to Rugby for 50 years and it was an appointment of considerable importance to the Society. Lee not only learnt from Arnold, maintaining the great classical tradition into the bargain, but inadvertently united a considerable circle of friends and colleagues who came to dominate the Society. In 1838 Lee was made Headmaster of King Edward's School, Birmingham, where he enjoyed huge success – unlike his time as first Bishop of Manchester. At King Edward's he encouraged a group of remarkable classical scholars: Edward White Benson, later Archbishop of Canterbury, Brooke Fosse Westcott and J.B. Lightfoot, both of whom became Bishop of Durham, Charles Evans, who later followed him as Head of King Edward's, C.B. Hutchinson and J.T. Pearse, who would be Headmaster of Birkenhead School. All these men, apart from Lightfoot, were to serve on the Committee, as did Lee, or on local committees, and gave very generously to the Society. Benson himself taught for a time at Rugby under Dr E.M. Goulbern, before going on to become the first Head of the newly founded Wellington College. During his time as schoolboy and schoolmaster he forged further links with others of like mind who went on to prominent positions where they could also bring their influence to bear. One such member of this extended group was T.W. Jex Blake, a boy at Rugby under Arnold, and then Head of both Cheltenham and Rugby before going on to be Dean of Wells. The result may have been what A.C. Benson[*] called 'well-groomed, well-mannered,

---

[*]   A.C. Benson was one of Edward White Benson's six children. He became an Eton Housemaster and then Master of Magdalene College, Cambridge.

36 F.W. Farrar, Dean of Canterbury, and formerly Master of Marlborough. His Eric; or Little by Little (1858) was popular but presented a picture of an earlier age.

37 A.P. Stanley, Dean of Westminster. An Old Rugbeian, his Life of Arnold (1844) reflected an era of Godliness and Good learning rather than later Muscular Christianity.

rational, manly boys, all taking the same view of things, all doing the same things,[7] conformists rather than individuals, but these men did bring an energy, drive and sense of social duty to a Society they served with distinction.

Of course, Arnold was not the only reformer of public schools, but he was the inspiration for others to follow. Several admired what he did at Rugby but disagreed totally with his political views and churchmanship. One such was G.H. Moberley, Headmaster of Winchester and later Bishop of Salisbury. Like the Wordsworths – Charles was the Headmaster of Winchester and then Bishop of St Andrew's while Christopher was Headmaster of Harrow before becoming Bishop of Lincoln – he was a High Churchman. These differences did not stop such men, or people like Benjamin Hall Kennedy or Samuel Butler, Kennedy's predecessor as Head of Shrewsbury, both classicists, from serving for long periods on the Society's Committees and organising regular collections from within their staffs.

Some might suggest that there was more than a little self-interest in this wide group of friends and colleagues and that they doubtless heeded the advice given by William Wilberforce to his son Samuel on his going up to Oxford, that social contacts might well prove useful in the future: 'Never omit any opportunity, my dear Sam, of getting acquainted with any good man, or useful man.'[8] While this may have been true, the Society certainly needed as much support as it could get. Samuel Wilberforce,

38   *Edward Thring, Old Etonian Headmaster of Uppingham, led the emphasis away from Godliness and Good Learning, and towards Muscular Christianity and greater efficiency. The latter in particular was reflected in the Society.*

Bishop of Oxford from 1845-69, was of the old school: a workaholic, he was beautifully mannered, energetic and ambitious, and 'he never lost sight of the spiritual in pursuing the temporal', wrote his friend Benjamin Jowett.* Wilberforce was in some respects like Blomfield, who, being high-handed and sarcastic and very conscious of his dignity (he even 'smiled episcopally'[9]), was considered the most unpopular bishop in the country in 1835, but both men were very able and fine public speakers, something the Society needed in the mid-century to engender support.

Yet none of these men was responsible for the Society taking a more forceful line in the second half of the 19th century. By the 1850s the atmosphere of Godliness and Good Learning which had produced the earnest and hard-working intellectual Victorian was passé.'Admirable in conscientiousness and moral fibre' though such men were, they were 'slightly ridiculous to succeeding generations.'[10] Society was changing considerably: the State was increasingly involved in parliamentary, educational and social reform, there were great changes in communications, improvements in medicine and science, and increasing challenges to Britain's worldwide dominance. The public schools needed to respond and as games and Muscular Christianity replaced Godliness and Good Learning, so the tradition of the schoolmaster-cleric slowly began to change too. The Society began to reflect this towards the last quarter of the century.

The turning point was marked by the publication of two books within a year of each other. In 1858 F.W. Farrar, Dean of Canterbury, published the bestselling novel of early Victorian school life, *Eric; or Little by Little*, which went through 36 editions during Farrar's lifetime. *Eric* reflects the moods of the 1830s rather than the 1850s, and the earlier *Life of Arnold* (1844) by Stanley had already given the reading public a view of Rugby at that time. It was *Tom Brown's Schooldays* (1857) by Thomas Hughes that made *Eric* appear absurd to those who had tired of Godliness and Good Learning. The book contained games, boyish spirits, manliness, and showed a school where sport was preferred to sermons. Arnold did leave his mark on his former pupil, Hughes, though, for the latter gave his enthusiastic support to F.D. Maurice and Christian Socialism, to Working Men's Associations and the Working Men's College. It was his social duty.

Tom Brown's Schooldays reflected the changes taking place in public schools. This change, perhaps surprisingly, was led by an Old Etonian. While not everybody had

---

* The Revd Benjamin Jowett, Master of Balliol and one of the seven contributors to *Essays and Reviews*, 1860; another contributor was a later Society President, Frederick Temple, Archbishop of Canterbury.

39 *George Ridding, Headmaster of Winchester, steered the society into calmer waters together with G.F.W. Mortimer and Montagu Butler.*

been unhappy at Keate's Eton – the Tractarian Edward Bouverie Pusey was not, but then he, like Christopher Wordsworth, 'had one foot in heaven and the other in the third century A.D.'[11] – Edward Thring certainly was. Thring's saving grace at Eton was that he was an outstanding games player, and as Headmaster of Uppingham he was determined to put into practice principles different from those knocked into him in the Long Chamber. It is true that E.C. Hawtrey and Francis Hodgson, then Headmaster and Provost respectively at Eton, tried to improve things after Keate, but in their own way and not according to the gospel of Arnold. 'Eton,' wrote Gladstone, 'was not sensibly affected by any influence extraneous to the place itself'. Thring, however, was determined to do things differently. He aimed to educate all pupils whatever their abilities, and to move towards Muscular Christianity by the introduction of compulsory games. His lead was followed by others and the make-up of the Society and Committee began to reflect his energy; the last quarter of the century saw the Committee dominated by another circle, this time of games players, all of whom had been at Eagle House in Hammersmith: George Ridding (later Head of Winchester), G.J. Blore (The King's School, Canterbury), E.C. Wickham (Wellington), Edmond Warre (Eton), and the hugely talented and generous Montagu Butler (Head of Harrow and later Master of Trinity College, Cambridge). All were still clerics, most were classicists, but all echoed Thring's desire for organised, disciplined care. It was they who helped the Society meet the challenges of the second half of the century, not least by taking a rather more forceful line.

8

A Degree of Adjustment

On 7 October 1849 Dr John Morris, Chairman since 1838 and a member since 1814, took charge of his last Committee meeting. By the end of the month he was dead. His son wrote to the Committee that his father had 'expressed a hope that he live no longer than he could be useful in the vineyard, and this wish was very nearly fulfilled ... only one Sunday intervened between his preaching to his flock and attending both services in church'[1] and his death.

Morris's death coincided with a difficult time for the Society. It lacked members, funds and ideas. The Annual Dinner had ceased in 1833 as, without royal support, too few attended, and so a useful source of donations ended. Too many had sat on the Committee for too long – Kelly lasted until 1835, Russell until 1863 – and so did their influence and opinions, and new blood was badly needed. Minutes of meetings indicate that little business was transacted; some meetings barely attracted a quorum. Few received relief. Attempts to increase membership and win public support continued along tried but trusted lines – a letter to headmasters, an advertisement in the press giving a list of patrons and subscribers, a circular to schools sent via the booksellers supplying them. Too much depended on grants made by such as the Cholmondely Fund or generous donations such as that of £1,000 by Mrs Sheppard in 1848. Some new blood did arrive – the Bishop of St Asaph, T.V. Short, became heavily involved, as did Christopher Wordsworth and E.C. Hawtrey, now Provost of Eton – but their ability to alter old established systems was, for some time, frustratingly small. Even E.W. Benson, who joined the Committee in 1843, could inject little life.

The loss of the Queen's support did hit the Society and in the 1850s funds were dangerously low. Despite the obvious problems, there were times when good business sense seems to have deserted the Committee and hearts ruled heads. In 1853 the Clergy Orphan Corporation wanted to establish a school for male orphans at Canterbury,[2] having received a bequest of £3,000 from a Captain Bean. This was subject to the dividends from the invested capital being paid to one of his relatives, Sophia Craig, during her lifetime or as long as she remained unmarried. The Society agreed to pay a sum equal to the dividends, about £90 per annum, so that the school might be built more quickly. This was really more than the Society could afford, however, and in 1854 it was proposed that there should be no further donations, but the proposal was defeated at the AGM of that year by four votes to three. The Committee then decided it would continue an annual subscription of £90 to the Corporation, who were highly delighted. By 1858 the Society was in real financial trouble, but an attempt at a Special Meeting to discontinue the grant failed. Instead it was reduced to £35 per annum. The Corporation said it was grateful for any support but would understand if, in the present circumstances, the Society decided to end its subscription. Eventually common sense prevailed and the grant was ended.

There were, fortunately, some positive straws in the wind. Individual members continued to support the objects of the Society as best they could: in 1860 the Royal Institute School, Liverpool, offered a free education to the sons of schoolmasters who properly qualified for support and, in 1874, the son of a Mrs Doria had his application accepted. In 1863 the Rules for Society Business were revised and approved. From the Society's point of view 1863 became a significant year. C.T. Longley, the new Archbishop of Canterbury,* became President at the invitation of the Treasurer, Russell, former Head of Charterhouse and a prominent member since 1810. It was Russell's last act for the Society, for he died soon afterwards. Significantly, at the first meeting after his demise, the Chairman, the Revd Thomas Spyers, 'submitted a series of emendations [which were carried] to the Rules … which he considered it desirable to adopt in consequence of the death of Dr Russell'.[3] Russell had kept the accounts very close to his chest; they needed to be sorted out and 'the Chairman, Treasurer [now Mortimer] and Auditors [had] an interview with Mr Francis Russell on the subject of his father's accounts'.[4] Following this a number of changes were introduced. Coutts and Co. replaced Child and Co. as the Society's bankers, and they immediately advised that the investments could be profitably moved about. Spare cash was more regularly invested and an updated list of subscribers drawn up.

40   *G.F.W. Mortimer, Headmaster of City of London School.*

The year also saw the death of another great servant of the Society, Archdeacon Charles Burney. He had been heavily involved since 1811 as Chairman, Auditor, Trustee and Vice-President. He received a fulsome tribute, having 'worked tirelessly when the Society was labouring under great difficulties [and having written] those eloquent appeals which were mainly instrumental in securing its position and permanency'. This may have been egging it a bit, and even a little optimistic given the

---

*   C.T. Longley had been Bishop of Ripon before being translated first to Durham and then to York and finally Canterbury. He had been a bishop since 1836 but started out as Headmaster of Harrow! Though a Low Churchman, he gave financial support to Nathaniel Woodard, founder of the the Anglo-Catholic Woodard Schools, as did Temple and Charles Kingsley: as the Society's Committee showed, churchmanship was not an obstacle to good works.

41 *Montagu Butler, Head of Harrow and later of Master of Trinity College, Cambridge.*

financial circumstances of the time, but there is no doubt that the Society owed men like Russell, Burney and Kelly an enormous debt. Equally certain is the fact that their influence lingered too long, their thinking being that of a former generation, and this was something which hampered the progress, and possibly the financial stability, of the Society.

A little movement was now possible. On paper, and increasingly in practice, the Officers of the Society constituted a formidable body: an archbishop, seven bishops, the Provosts of Eton and King's College, Cambridge, the Revd Richard Okes, and the heads of major schools among them. From the 1860s onwards there is a greater sense of purposeful commitment. Investments were constantly reviewed, with the

Revd Dr G.F.W. Mortimer consulting not just with Coutts but also with the Stock Exchange, and even though the Committee eventually rejected the suggestion, they were persuaded to consider seriously investing in something that was still relatively new – the railways. However, neither English Railway stock nor that of the Indian Railway was deemed safe enough! The network of local representatives, which included the wonderfully helpful Revd Francis Kilvert* as agent for the Bath area, was expanded into a network of local committees covering the whole country. These were able to put a little more pressure on schools and their staffs to help swell the funds, and for several years these donations were a major source of income.

By 1871 confidence was much restored and though the Society was never wealthy it claimed it was able to help an increasing number of applicants.† This improvement was in part due to the hard work of the Treasurer, Mortimer, Headmaster of the City of London School, who died that year having 'placed the Society in a position of prosperity and usefulness which it had never before attained'. He had increased the Society's Funded Property from £7,700 to £10,000 in the nine years he had acted as Treasurer. His widow, Jane, replying on 28 September 1871 to the Society's letter of condolence, conveyed the feelings of all Committee members when she wrote of her husband: 'he warmly felt the sorrow of each distressed applicant'. The Society was now in much better shape to meet the challenges of a changing Britain. So that as much as possible could be given in relief, Mortimer had insisted on keeping working expenses to a minimum – even so a member of the Harrow Common Room complained that the Society's Secretary, Octavian Blewitt, an Old Etonian, got too generous a salary (£50 per annum). In practice a very tight rein was kept on expenditure and the Collector, one Pellatt, soon to be sacked, was refused commission of £1 10s. 6d. until he could satisfactorily account to the Treasurer for his claim for eight shillings for postage and stationery.

A random glance at the Committee of the 1870s shows a mixture of strands – the heads of seven of the nine ancient public schools are present, and the traditions of classicism, Arnold and Thring are to be seen respectively in Benson, Vaughan and Kennedy, and Butler and Ridding. The men who guided the Society through the 19th century shared links and aims: social duty may not have been a phrase which entered heads in 1797, but something not dissimilar had inspired the founders too.

---

*   The Revd Francis Kilvert: see his *Diaries*, which have become very popular. He was a typical product of the mid-19th century – sentimental, pious, respectable and quite free from humbug. The world he described may attract modern readers but was in fact one of great poverty.
†   The increase was hardly dramatic: the number helped went up from 23 to 27, though the mid-1880s did see numbers get into the low forties.

9

Relief:
A Period of Relative Calm

It is beyond the scope of this work to consider in any depth the political, social and economic changes that occurred in Britain and the world in general during the 19th and 20th centuries. An outline of some must suffice. The population of Britain was growing rapidly – about 13 million in 1815, it had doubled by 1871 and by 1901 had reached 42 million, though by then the birth rate was slowing. In 1815 the majority of the population worked in agriculture, but only 30 years later nearly half lived in towns and cities, where heavy industries flourished, fuelled by the growth of steam power and the building of factories. Communications, especially by rail, became far easier. But the move to towns and cities came at a price – slums, dirt, appalling working conditions and misery were abundant. In the towns and cities, rich and poor were kept apart: the poor, for example, were not allowed into London's Piccadilly and the squares and streets of Mayfair were gated against them.

Eventually Parliament, whose power increased as that of the monarchy weakened, produced a series of reforms which led to the social services and the apparatus of the state as we know it today – though, of course, much of this change took place in the 20th century. Change in the 19th century was helped by the long period of peace that Britain enjoyed in Europe: from 1815 to 1914 there was no involvement in European war, except in the Crimea from 1854-6. But although Britain enjoyed a period of 'peace' in Europe, there were disturbances in Jamaica, Canada, Ceylon (Sri Lanka), South Africa and Ireland, and the Mutiny of 1857 was only part of a series of uprisings in India.

There had been very little progress towards either a national system of education or old age pensions before 1867.* The first grant of public money – £20,000 for the building of schools – had in fact been made in 1833, and there had been a recommendation for local education boards in 1858, but it was the 1867 Reform Act that provided the real impetus for the setting up of a national system of free and compulsory education. The 1870 Education Act provided local school boards with the powers to make education compulsory up to the age of 13, and in 1918 education

---

* When Victoria, early in her reign, had asked Melbourne about the desirability of educating the poor, he had replied, 'Why bother the poor? Leave them alone.'

in all elementary schools was made free. As for pensions, the 1908 Liberal Budget provided a limited start, and in 1911 the National Insurance Act signalled that the state had accepted the need to provide for people's welfare out of the public purse. In time all this was to make an impact on the work of the Society.

It is true that by 1900 standards of living for much of the population were slowly beginning to improve, and by 1914 most people were better clothed, fed and housed, but this was not the case everywhere. Factors such as falling prices and growing worldwide competition had hit agriculture very hard in the 1880s.

For the Society it was a period of relative calm, and the time was used to tighten procedures and revise the Rules to take account of developments taking place on the wider scale – in 1883 an amendment allowed assistance to be given to masters 'of all schools not coming under the Elementary Education Act, their widows and orphans'[1] who had been teaching for at least five years. This better organised and more business-like Society was able to work up to the end of the First World War without much obvious fuss. The nearest thing to excitement came at the turn of the century. Previously only the Church's Kalendar had moved meetings of the Society, but in 1901 things were different: the General Meeting scheduled for 2 February was adjourned until the following week 'owing to the funeral of Her Majesty Queen Victoria'[2] and in 1902 the Committee moved its scheduled meeting of 25 October to 18 October 'because of the Royal Progress.'[3] Other Society-shattering events included the appointment of professional Auditors in 1904 and the acceptance of an offer by Coutts to cut their commission by 50 per cent.

In 1904 W.G. Rushbrooke, then teaching at City of London School but later to become both Headmaster of St Olave's, Southwark and Chairman, tried to persuade the Board of Education to create a pension fund for all assistant masters. He failed, which went to show that the Society no longer had the clout it had had in 1797. It is true that pension schemes were available in some schools – probably the first were introduced by the Woodard Corporation – but these were not widespread. Nor did masters teaching in private schools make much use of the schemes on the open market – they were not cheap. When a national scheme was introduced following the 1908 Budget, the Society advised several who had applied for relief, such as Edward Griffith, to apply instead for an old age pension. The introduction of state pensions also brought a problem of sorts to all charities; relief had to be limited, and in some cases declined, as it was to John Robinson, because to make a grant 'would entail the forfeiture of his old age pension.'[4]

Such restrictions meant that charities had to be very careful in their grants and had to work together to ensure they did not cause additional problems for the recipient. They had also to guard against possible fraud. By 1900 the Society was already working closely with several organisations: some, such as the Clergy Orphan Corporation and the Charity Organisation Society, had been involved with the Society for many years. Not surprisingly, and this was possibly a little reassuring to the Committee, some of these charities encountered similar financial difficulties to those experienced by the Society. In 1903 the Charity Organisation Society was writing to the Society about a man who had died leaving a balance of £7 15s. from

THE HEAD MASTERS' CONFERENCE.

The annual Conference of Head Masters met this year at University College, London. The meeting commenced yesterday, and will be concluded to-day. The Conference first assembled at Uppingham in 1869, and its meetings have since been held at Rugby, Marlborough, Harrow, Eton, Wellington, Dulwich, Sherborne, Highgate &c. It is a meeting " of the head masters of the highest schools, to discuss all questions affecting schools and education." At yesterday's meeting the head masters of the following schools were present :—Abingdon, Rev. E. Summers ; Bedford, Mr. J. S. Phillpotts ; Berkhampstead, Rev. E. Bartrum ; Birkenhead, Rev. J. T. Pearse ; Birmingham (King Edward's School), Rev. A. R. Vardy ; Blackheath, Rev. E. W. South ; Brecon, Rev. D. Lewis Lloyd ; Brighton ·College, Rev. T. Hayes Belcher ; Bromsgrove, Mr. H. Millington ; Bury St. Edmund's, Mr. J. Sankey ; Cambridge (Perse School), Mr. J. B. Allen ; Canterbury (King's School), Rev. G. J. Blore, D.D. ; Cheltenham College, Rev. H. Kynaston ; Clifton College, Rev. J. M. Wilson ; Cranbrook, Rev. C. Crowden ; Dulwich College, Rev. A. J. Carver, D.D. ; Durham, Rev. W. A. Fearon ; Eastbourne College, Rev. Thompson Podmore ; Felstead, Rev. D. S. Ingram ; Giggleswick, Rev. G. Style ; Heversham, Rev. W. Hart ; Highgate, Rev. C. M'Dowall ; Ipswich, Rev. H. A. Holden, LL.D. ; Liverpool Royal Institution, Rev. H. J. Johnson ; City of London, Rev. E. A. Abbott, D.D. ; International College, Mr. H. R. Ladell ; King's College, Rev. T. Stokoe, D.D. ; Mill-hill (N.W.), Mr. R. F. Weymouth, D.Lit. ; Southwark (St. Olave's), Rev. J. Johnson ; University College School, Mr. H. W. Eve ; Malvern College, Rev. C. T. Cruttwell ; Marlborough College, Rev. G. C. Bell ; Newcastle (Staffordshire), Mr. F. E. Kitchener ; Newport (Salop), Mr. T. Collins ; Norwich, Rev. C. W. Tancock ; Oswestry, Mr. M. S. Forster ; Oundle, Rev. H. St. John Reade ; Radley (St. Peter's College), Rev. R. J. Wilson ; Rossall (Fleetwood), Rev. H. A. James ; Rugby, Rev. T. W. Jex-Blake, D.D. ; Sherborne. Rev. E. M. Young ; Shrewsbury, Rev. H. W. Moss ; Sutton Valence, Rev. J. D. Kingdon ; Tonbridge, Rev. T. B. Rowe ; Uppingham, Rev. E. Thring ; Wellington College, Rev. E. C. Wickham ; Wolverhampton, Mr. T. Beach ; Worcester (Cathedral School), Rev. W. E. Bolland.

setting definite books for translation in public examinations and replacing them by unseen translations only."

Dr. Abbott seconded the motion, and said that many boys appeared to pass an examination in Cicero and Virgil, but really knew nothing of the Latin language.

Dr. Butler's amendment was then carried.

The Rev. E. Bartram urged the claims of the Society of Schoolmasters to the support of the Conference.

Mr. Thring moved, " That the Conference considers it desirable that the members should make more widely known the claims of the Society of Schoolmasters on the support of all schools represented at the Conference." He advised that a sub-committee should be appointed, with Mr. Bartram to make suggestions, to be brought either before the Committee of the Conference or the Committee of the Schoolmasters' Society.

Mr. Wilson seconded the motion, and it was carried.

The Rev. G. C. Bell gave some explanations respecting the report and statement of finance.

The Conference then adjourned until this morning at 10 o'clock.

The Head Master (Mr. Eve) of University College School entertained the members of the Conference and other distinguished guests at a dinner in the library of University College. Among those present were Mr. Justice Fry, the Dean of Westminster, Mr. Erichsen, Sir A. Hobhouse, the Master of University College, Oxford, Mr. Oscar Browning, Sir G. Young, Mr. Cozens-Hardy, and nearly all the professors of the College.

In the evening a *conversazione* was given by the Council of the College and the Head Master of the School in the Flaxman Gallery.

By the invitation of the Rev. Dr. Abbott and the committee, members of the Conference will visit the new buildings of the City of London School on the Embankment to-day between 2 and 4.

42   *Attempts were made to involve HMC more positively in the Society, as this report in* The Times *of 22 December 1882 shows.*

the grant of £13 (5s. a week) made by the Society. 'I hold it,' wrote COS's Secretary, 'pending your instructions. I may perhaps mention that our funds are sadly in need of more support, and if your Committee can kindly see its way to place said balance to the swelling of such funds, we should indeed be very grateful.'[5] But, sadly, the Society couldn't. The Society also worked increasingly closely with the Professional Classes Aid Council and in 1921 was invited to nominate a representative (A.A. Somerville) to that organisation's Committee, something which has continued. The Council also put together a Central Register of applicants, an idea which was welcomed by the Society and supplied details and information about those it had dealt with. Other charities with which the Society worked include the Sons of the Clergy, the Clergy Widows Fund, the Aged Poor Society, the Guild of Aid for Gentlefolk and the Royal

43 *Bishop Percival of Hereford.*

44 *Edwin Abbott, former Headmaster of City of London School, succeeded Percival at the age of eighty.*

United Kingdom Beneficent Association. Some charities were very small and specific, such as Hawkey's Charity, the Hetherington Charity for the Blind, and A Charity for Masters who are communicants of the Church of England. In the future the Society would continue to work with others.

There remained the need to increase the Charitable Fund – and from as many different sources as possible. Traditional appeals continued, sometimes targeted at particular areas such as the preparatory schools, and local committees and headmasters sought to involve their schools and staffs. In 1890, for example, the Heads of Radley, Rossall, King's College School and University College School declared that their establishments would contribute to the Fund, and others followed their lead. This was more generous than might appear at first sight: many schools, especially in London, were in considerable difficulty in the 1880s and 1890s.

The Headmasters' Conference (HMC) was not so easy to trap. The Revd G.H. Rendall, Head of Charterhouse and Vice-President of the Society, wrote somewhat stuffily on behalf of HMC in 1905, that it could 'not be used to promote the Society as it would set a precedent, but since the next Conference would be outside London, the host might then quite appropriately and more effectually use the occasion to bring the Society informally before the notice of all present.'[6] Why it mattered whether the conference was held in or out of London is not certain! Nevertheless, HMC had occasionally contributed since 1887, and continued to do so from time to time, giving sums of between £20 and £100, until in 1925 it agreed an annual contribution of £50, though this was to change. Governing bodies occasionally donated – that of St Olave's Grammar School gave £63 – and there were some generous donations from livery companies, notably the Merchant Taylors', Mercers' and Skinners'. One idea, which might have proved beneficial, if only because of people's neglecting to cancel it, came from a Committee member, the Revd Walter Chipper (Head of the Lower School and Assistant Chaplain at Christ's College, Finchley), who suggested that subscribers be given the option of completing a banker's order. But it fell on deaf ears.

So for most of this period the Society trundled on, never rich but not in danger of collapse either. In some respects things didn't change at all. From 1915 the much loved President, the Bishop of Hereford, Dr Percival, tried to retire on the grounds of old age, then ill-health, then both. All were refused. Each year the Minutes recorded: 'A letter was read from the Bishop of Hereford. The Bishop of Hereford was re-elected unanimously.'[7] In 1918 he got his way by dying! He was succeeded by the 80-year-old Revd Dr Edwin Abbott, former Head of City of London School and a member since 1862.

10

Help!

It might be supposed that the effects of national and world events would be reflected in the numbers applying for relief. While undoubtedly events did affect members, there is little evidence of this happening until the second half of the 19th century, when the records become more complete and changes in education and then the First World War finally take their toll. Other charities seem to have been hit harder than the Society: in 1884, the Clergy Orphan Corporation appealed to the Committee for financial help as 'these are hard times for us. We feel most seriously the effects of the prevailing agricultural depression, and are more than ever dependant [*sic*] on Societies and Corporations'.[1] The Society replied that it was not within its Rules to make any grants to another charitable society. There were, of course, many reasons why people applied to the Society for help, but for most of the 19th century the effects of death, illness and insanity dominate the case histories.

Entries in the early years are often very brief: 'Mr James Giles – a lunatic formerly a schoolmaster'[2] is not untypical. Brevity, however, did not mean lack of interest: the Giles family, for instance, was supported for 31 years. All applicants had to be subscribers and be supported in their application. It was not easy at the start of the 19th century to get accurate information about claimants, and though the Society tried hard to vet people, mistakes were made. For perfectly understandable reasons, reliance sometimes had to be placed on the word of those known to the Committee: Mr Lawes of Chippingham was recommended 'by our worthy President, the Bishop of Gloucester' and the Revd J. Reynolds was 'supported by Lord Chesterfield and our zealous friend Thos Hammersley'.[3] We are not told what had gone wrong for these unfortunates. In 1812, 10 guineas was awarded to a 'celebrated mathematician under confinement in consequence of mental indisposition, occasioned by too close an application to professional studies. From motives of prudence towards him, his name was not announced: his wife is pregnant and had five children'.[4] It would be intriguing to know more of these, and similar, cases but the details are thin. It is not until 1835 that greater information is provided, and then it is only addresses and the names of referees; only from 1865 did applicants have to provide more financial detail.

Whether or not the Committee thought of St James' instruction to come 'to the help of orphans and widows when they need it' is unknown, but this is certainly what

98

Rev. J. W. P. Jones, M.A. Age 35. Single. Educated at Brackley Dec. 1862 10
now in Warneford Asylum Northamptonshire & Worcester College Oxford. Dec. 1863 10
Oxford. Assistant Master in the Clergy Orphan School
Canterbury, & in several private schools.
[died Apl. 1864] Dependent on his Brother & Sister. Auth. of Rev.
Dr. Major &c.

Miss Charity Archer Age 13. Orphan of Mr. Thomas Andrew Archer, Dec. 1862 25
1. Richmond Terrace B.A. Trin: Coll: Dublin, who was Educated at towards her Education
Shelton Stoke upon Trent Chelmsford Gr. Sch. and kept a Boarding School Oct. 1863 25
at Shelton Hall N. Stoke upon Trent. He died Apl. 1864 25 to be final
in 1853, & his widow died in 1862. Recommended
by Rev. S. Bartrum of Hertford Sch. & others

Rev. John Wm. Hewett, Age 38. Married, 5 children under 6 y's. Dec. 1862 10
Sutton Educated at Barnstaple Gr. Sch. & Trin: Coll. Camb. Dec. 1865 20
Burton on Trent. April. Master of Bloxham Grammar School Dec. 1866 10
*the grant was made without Oxon, from 1853 to 1857, since then taking private Dec. 1878 10
the Committee being informed pupils
at rather being kept in
ignorance of his impending
bankruptcy, which took
place within a fortnight
of the grant being made -
Dec. Standles of Dec.
22. 1078.

45   *A page from the Relief Book.*

they did! Throughout the century, widows continued to be left with large families and little to live on: Mrs Elwell of Sevenoaks, aged 42, was a widow with 10 children between 15 years and nine months of age and her only income was £8 a year; in 1832 Mrs Shapcott was left with 11 children, nine of whom were dependent on her. She was helped for 10 years by the Society, which also paid her legal bill when a relative tried to defraud one of her sons who was taken to court. Several widows did what they could to help themselves: one such was Helen Jackson, who was left with nine children and 'endeavours to support herself by needlework and letting rooms.'[5] Not all were widows: Adolphe Ragon and his seven offspring were supported both in the 1890s and again between 1924 and 1936. He was only one of several who were helped over a long period – Mrs Jane Bateman received aid between 1812 and 1860. It was extremely difficult to extricate oneself from the poverty trap.

Sometimes it was rather unexpected people who found themselves seeking help. Mrs Scott was the daughter of the Prince of Neufchatel's brother.[6] The Revd Dr William Lonsdale was one of several who had been educated at Eton and Cambridge and had been a Headmaster. The Revd J.R. Major, Headmaster of King's College School, Auditor of the Society and Committee member, was very generous to the Society but seemingly less so to his family, more than one of whom had to apply for relief. Another Committee member, Trollope, failed likewise and his son, who also taught at Christ's Hospital, died at the age of 49 in 1846, leaving a wife and eight children destitute. Many came from privileged backgrounds but blindness, insanity,

SOCIETY OF SCHOOLMASTERS,

FOR THE RELIEF OF DISTRESSED SCHOOLMASTERS AND USHERS, AND OF THEIR WIDOWS AND ORPHANS.

Instituted 1798, and Maintained by Voluntary Contributions.

PRESIDENT.
HIS GRACE THE ARCHBISHOP OF CANTERBURY.

HONORARY PRESIDENTS.

The LORD BISHOP OF LONDON.
The LORD BISHOP OF EXETER.
The LORD BISHOP OF LINCOLN.

The LORD BISHOP OF SALISBURY.
The LORD BISHOP OF BARBADOS.

VICE-PRESIDENTS.

Right Hon. J. R. MOWBRAY, M.P.
Right Hon. Sir WILLIAM HEATHCOTE, Bart.
Very Rev. the DEAN OF PETERBOROUGH.
Very Rev. the DEAN OF CHRISTCHURCH.
Very Rev. the DEAN OF NORWICH.
Rev. CANON KENNEDY, D.D.
Rev. CANON WESTCOTT, D.D.
Ven. ARCHDEACON JENNINGS, M.A.
Ven. ARCHDEACON BALSTON, D.D.
Rev. CHANCELLOR BENSON.

Rev. the PROVOST OF ETON.
Rev. the PROVOST OF KING'S.
Rev. Dr. VAUGHAN, D.D., Master of the Temple.
Sir WILLOUGHBY JONES, Bart.
Professor BONAMY PRICE, M.A.
Rev. Professor PRITCHARD, M.A., F.R.A.S.
BENJAMIN BOND CABBELL, Esq., M.A., F.R.S.
GEORGE MOORE, Esq.
Alderman FINNIS.
JOHN P. GASSIOT, Esq., F.R.S.

TRUSTEES.

Rev. CANON BARRY, D.D.
Rev. CHARLES BRODRICK SCOTT, D.D.

Ven. ARCHDEACON BROWNE, M.A.
Rev. EVAN EDWARD ROWSELL, M.A.

ACTING COMMITTEE.

Rev. THOMAS SPYERS, D.D., Weybridge, *Chairman.*
Rev. E. ABBOTT ABBOTT, D.D., City of London School.
Rev. J. A. L. AIREY, M.A., MerchantTaylors' School.
Rev. GEORGE C. BELL, M.A., Christ's Hospital.
Rev. E. H. BRADBY, M.A., Haileybury College.
Rev. W. HAIG BROWN, LL.D., Charter-house School, Godalming.
Rev. R. W. BUSH, M.A., Islington Proprietary School.
Rev. H. MONTAGU BUTLER, D.D., Harrow School.
Rev. ALFRED J. CARVER, D.D., Dulwich College.
Rev. JAMES COOPER, M.A., 27, Woburn Square.
Rev. J. B. DYNE, D.D., late of Highgate School.
Rev. JAMES J. HORNBY, D.D., Eton College.

Rev. B. F. JAMES, M.A., Westminster School.
Rev. T. W. JEX-BLAKE, D.D., Rugby.
Rev. J. KEMPTHORNE, M.A., Blackheath Proprietary School.
Rev. HERBERT KYNASTON, D.D., St. Paul's School.
Rev. G. F. MACLEAR, D.D., King's College School.
Rev. JAMES MARSHALL, M.A., Westminster School.
Rev. G. B. F. POTTICARY, M.A., Girton Rectory, near Cambridge.
Rev. GEORGE RIDDING, D.D., Winchester College.
Rev. CANON WELLDON, D.C.L., Tunbridge School.
Rev. W.D. WEST, D.D., Epsom College.
And the Treasurer and Auditors.

TREASURER.
Rev. W. BAKER, D.D., Merchant Taylors' School.

BANKERS.
Messrs. COUTTS & Co., 59, Strand.

AUDITORS.
Rev. JOSEPH H. LUPTON, M.A., St. Paul's School.
Rev. R.WHITTINGTON, M.A., Merchnt. Taylors' Schl.

SECRETARY.
OCTAVIAN BLEWITT, Esq., K.L., F.R.G.S., 10, John Street, Adelphi, W.C.

The SOCIETY OF SCHOOLMASTERS was established in 1798 for the relief of necessitous Masters, Ushers, and Assistants of Endowed, Proprietary, and Boarding Schools, their Widows and Orphans, Members of the Society having the first claim to consideration.

The Rules provide that the Members of the Society shall be Schoolmasters and others who shall be Donors of not less than £5. 5s. in one sum, or shall subscribe not less than £1. 1s. annually, for five successive years, or not less than 10s. 6d. annually, for ten successive years. The Committee, in cases of distress, advanced age, or infirmity, have power to make grants of not more than £50 to Members, their Widows and Orphans, and of not more than £25 to Non-Members, their Widows and Orphans, provided that the space of twelve months at least intervene between two consecutive grants.

The sum distributed by the Committee in relief during the past 34 years has been £10,234, and has been steadily increasing in amount, the grants of the first 10 years of that period having been £2,988, while the grants of the last 10 years have been £3,093.

The Committee submit these facts to the members of the Profession, and, at the same time, earnestly solicit the attention of the Public to the necessities of afflicted and meritorious Schoolmasters.

They confidently hope that those who have enjoyed the blessings derived from education, will not be unmindful of the services rendered to society by men who faithfully devote to the instruction of the young the vigour of their life, and the laborious exercise of their best faculties.

Subscriptions and Donations are received by the Treasurer, the Rev. Dr. Baker, D.D., Merchant Taylors' School, E.C.; by the Secretary, 10, John Street, Adelphi, W.C.; and by the Members of the Acting Committee.

The Committee meet at the Chambers of the Royal Literary Fund, No. 10, John Street, Adelphi, Strand, on the first Saturday of February, October, and December, and on the last Saturday of April, at Two o'clock.

Forms of Application for relief may be obtained at No. 10, John Street, Adelphi, W.C.

46 *Early advertising material from the end of the 19th century.*

paralysis, consumption and apoplectic fits did not respect privilege. Some things were, however, self-induced: 'bed-ridden and suffering from spinal paralysis due to drink' was just one such example.

Many of the applicants were young by today's standards: between 1855 and 1860, for instance, 57 per cent were under fifty years old. Victorian healthcare was poor by modern standards, but many were simply victims of circumstance. Mary Woolley was left a widow when her husband went down with the SS *London*.[7] Charles de Langhe served as a captain in the Engineers during the Franco-Prussian War of 1869-71[8] but damaged his eyesight and was unable to return to teaching. Mrs Charlotte Rowney and her husband had been well-off but had 'lost all on a farm in Devon when he was burnt out by Wreckers, against whom he had given information at Lloyds'.[9] Herr Richard Teutschel, 32, had to resign from positions he had held in good schools because of an illness for which 'he has been advised to try the water cure at Malvern', something which either worked or killed him, for he didn't apply again! The Revd W. Heaton of Bridgnorth in Shropshire 'lost his savings in investments but drew his living (£121) from Glebe income' in 1888. He was not the only one to be distressed as a result of speculation; so also was the Revd William Atkinson, educated at Marlborough and Oxford and Headmaster of Salisbury School, who had 'lost his private income through the depreciation of Buenos Ayars [*sic*] Bonds'. And there was Frederick William Frith, who 'had to go into the workhouse' in 1911.

A sizeable group of those the Society helped had been affected by growing competition, either from new public schools or the establishment of National Board Schools. There were too many private schools, many of which found themselves wrongly placed as towns spread out, and most struggled for pupils and hence fees, and were unable to improve their schools as a result. 'Only seven boarders' and 'ten to eighteen boarders', 'only one pupil' are all common entries. Mark Antony Lower, master of a boarding school in Lewes from 1837 to 1867, was married with six children and applied in distress because of 'failing health and the injury done to his school by the establishment of numerous colleges in Sussex'. Ernest Pennington had his school 'ruined by the establishment of St Dunstan's School, Catford', and Edward Gardener, who lived in Old Kent Road, lost his school at Walworth in 1889 following the introduction of the London School Board – such Boards leading to the collapse of several schools. As a result his means of support was 'occasional private teaching and sign writing. Does not earn more than 1/- a day'. So it was for others: 'competition of other schools' and 'of rate supported schools', or 'deprived of his school in 1886 by the opening of the High School in Notting Hill' are typical entries.

Some claimants were clearly not cut out for the job. Anthony Lucy was dismissed 'for hopeless interference'; Theobald Swift 'had twelve jobs between 1884 and 1906, three years of which were spent at Durham University'; George Ingram, who sold his school in Croydon for £90, was described as 'an absteeming man, but perhaps a little lacking in energy'; de Winton 'retired owing to ill-health and fear of getting into debt' – although that fear didn't stop him getting there. He was refused help, but not the others. Most cases were just sad: 70-year-old John Newsom was 'unable to earn a living from age and a fractured hip, his sole income being 2s. a week from a will and 4s. a week from private tuition'; the Wilkinson sisters of Durham were 'left only furniture by their parents and doctors' bills, not yet paid off'; nor were they paid by the Society. For some the sale of their furniture was the only thing left to them before they applied to the Society, something they did reluctantly, and at the cost of their self-esteem: Frederick Lowe's 'only source of support was the proceeds of sale of furniture'. There was clearly great hardship, seen in entries like '£4 for dentures' and '£10 for clothing, so that he may take up his appointment'; similar entries continue well into the 20th century.

Some fell into poverty through sheer bad luck or through the fault of others. William Henry Crippin lost everything when Sankey, Flint and Co., Solicitors in Canterbury, were themselves ruined in 1885, and Mrs Emmeline Sweetlove, a widow for 35 years, had 'lost her property by the speculation of a Trustee, who now agrees to pay her 5/- a week [but it is] very irregularly paid; earns 4/- or 5/- a week by needlework'. Robert Clough was undone by illness: 'in 1881 scarlet fever broke out in his school and he had to mortgage his furniture'. Charles Carreck became distressed 'due to loss of pupils through the bankruptcy of clients and parents not paying fees' – and that was in Royal Tunbridge Wells! Arthur Richard Leetham's difficulties may have been the result of an Act of God. Leetham, 43, was married with four children and was 'just on the point of selling his school at Winchester, where numbers had decreased, partly owing to his having become a Roman Catholic, when diphtheria broke out' and he was forced 'to sign his petition in bankruptcy'. But perhaps James Webb Bailey of Hammersmith was the most unlucky of all. He was already receiving some help from the Mercers' Company when he applied to the Society for additional support, which he got. However, he needed further help when he had 'his skull fractured by an electric car on 13 April 1901'. Sadly the Society's aid did him little good for he died in St Thomas's Hospital 11 weeks later.

Not all cases were straightforward. George Cumming, 43, ran a private school in Tonbridge but was 'ruined by an unjust prosecution for punishing a boy who had assaulted one of his female pupils, when though acquitted, he had to pay his own costs', and Victor Cerexhe, a Frenchman, put his troubles down to losing his post (at University College School) and the cost of prosecuting a bigamist who had married his daughter. Both were rejected by the Committee. Over some there was disagreement at the highest level. Mr Samuel Luckman had taught Archbishop Benson's sons and Benson supported his application. The Society gave him help in 1887 and again in 1906, when the President and Bishop of Hereford, Percival, informed the Committee that 'Mr Luckman [was] utterly unworthy of help'. He got no further aid.

One or two claimants clutched at straws. Joseph Herbert Ingram had taught until 1896 but for a year since then 'had been canvassing for a tea firm and brewery'. He wished now 'to start a poultry farm'. Others were lucky for a time. Grimwood Offord came from Ham in Surrey and received help for 25 years, until the Secretary made enquiries and was told by the vicar that 'Mr Offord is unworthy of assistance, being frequently drunk and uses objectionable language'. Some didn't deserve – or get – any aid. The widow of George Stignall was rejected because she was 'a confirmed drunkard, now in the lowest depths of shame and degradation'. Thomas Hillman was just ungrateful: he had run out of pupils and was given £10, only to complain to Dr Warre, former Headmaster of Eton and an Honorary President and who did not know him, 'holding up the Society to reprobation for giving him so small a sum'. It didn't stop Hillman from trying on five further occasions, and being rejected on each. The Revd Henry Dodwell didn't deserve financial help either. He was 51 in 1877, with four children under nine. He had been a headmaster but, according to him, had been turned out of two schools as a result of 'false returns without enquiry by the Local Government Board'. He later attempted to shoot the Master of the Rolls. Tried and convicted, he was sent to Broadmoor Asylum as insane and died there in 1900.

Some cases pose questions of interest to the 21st century: Ralph Dadge was 38 and musical and he taught in some good private schools before becoming 'organist at the private chapel at Balmoral from 1895 to 1902. His wife is a daughter of John Brown, Queen Victoria's servant'. Other cases still ring a bell today. Albert Leathley lost his school because parents of the pupils wanted to interfere with the management and objected to a term's fees being claimed in lieu of notice.

There is an element of sadness in all these cases and a hint of desperation in several of them. The Committee did its best to be fair to every applicant. It gave nothing, however, to Walter Kaye of Harrogate, who applied in 1908. Kaye's application listed as the causes of his distress 'competition – over 50 private schools in Harrogate, ill-health, robbery, depreciation of shares, bad debts, loss through law suit'. His case embraced most of the reasons why people applied – and suggests why some were rejected.

The First World War made an immediate impact on schools and teachers and many of the cases dealt with by the Society were referred to it by the Cabinet sub-Committee of the National Relief Fund. Some cases refer to events with which students of the First World War will be familiar, some to the after-effects of the conflict. John Edward Jones, Principal of a school in Birkenhead, was the first to come to the Committee's attention, having 'lost his pupils owing to the war'. He was rapidly followed by George Fisher of Folkestone, William Rugg of the Nautical Academy in East London, and Albert Cole from Clifton, all of whom 'lost [their] pupils at the outbreak of war'. Kenneth Randall had been teaching at Chigwell School for several years when, in 1914, he bought a school in Fareham and began 'with every prospect of success. The war had ruined his school'. John Matthew Abbott, aged 69, also lost his pupils due to the war and then had 'a stroke of paralysis'. He and his wife went to Bedford Poor Law Institution, from which they rapidly discharged themselves. The Society looked after them, as far as it was able, from 1916 to 1935. Another teacher who had lost pupils because of the war was John Storey, who died aged 61: the Society helped his widow, who was earning £1 a week making sphagnum moss.

Some who taught abroad were similarly affected. Henry Prebble was 69 and had been teaching in Switzerland until the outbreak of war, which resulted in the loss of his pupils and forced him to return to England where he was supported by the Society until 1929 as he was unable to find a job. Ernest Maitland was a little luckier. He had taught in Switzerland and lost his pupils, too, but returned to England and found employment at Wellesley House School in Broadstairs, although his wife was an invalid and had to remain in Switzerland with their daughter. Maitland was 57 and had previously been in the Church.

Just as pupils responded to the war effort, doubtless anticipating that it would be over by Christmas, so several masters enlisted in 1914, determined to serve their country. Frederick Wellwood, 59, of Dundee, was a headmaster in Lanarkshire when war broke out. By October 1914 he had been commissioned into the 9th Battalion Border Regiment and from there into a service battalion, the 10th Royal Lancashires. At this stage, however, he was declared unfit for active duties and asked to resign. He was referred to the Society by the Government Committee on Relief of Distress, but then became Recruiting Officer

A TALE OF DISTRESS.—*Emily Pizzey*, a young woman, who had a careworn and destitute appearance, was charged with begging from house to house at Queen's-gate, Kensington, by means of a begging letter. —The Prisoner was first brought before Mr. Sheil on Wednesday, when he remanded her for one day for inquiry.—Inspector Jackson said he went to 114, London-wall, where he found that the Prisoner and her husband had been living about three months. There was not any furniture in the room—neither chair, table, nor bed. The Prisoner and her husband slept on the floor. He was informed that they had not had any food for three days. He also found that the husband had kept a college at Brockley, but was unsuccessful. He was a man of good education, and could speak several languages.—The Prisoner's Husband was called forward and asked by the Magistrate why he did not apply to the parish if he was in distress.—The Husband said he took a lodging in the City in the hope of being able to recover his position. He had parted with everything, and he had paid for advertisements for situations when his children wanted food. He had two children at home with no one to look after them. He was educated for the Church.—Mr. Paget said he should like to have some inquiry made by the Charity Organisation Society, and remanded the Prisoner, taking the husband's recognisances for her appearance.

47   The Times, *October 1866: the desperate straits of the Pizzey family.*

at Dundee on 11s. 7d. a day. Later he was again referred to the Society, this time by the Cabinet sub-Committee of the National Relief Fund. Hugh Robert Mapleston, aged 38, immediately 'rejoined his old Corps, the Artists' Rifles, on the outbreak of war, but he was discharged about a month later as medically unfit'. Hugh Augustus Morris seems to have been poorly treated: he enlisted in the University Brigade, Royal Fusiliers, but was 'discharged from the Army owing to a badly strained heart, without any grant of any kind'. Such men may not have got to the Front, but still sacrificed a great deal.

Some did go to war. Madame Marie Ruf, from Vienne in France, saw her husband, a Professor at the Royal Military College, Sandhurst,[*] go off to the Front in 1914. In March 1918 he was declared missing at Noyon, leaving his wife in need of support from the Society. Help was also given to the widow of Albert Fitzgerald, who died in September 1918 at the age of 39. He had been 'taken prisoner when the war broke out and remained so until he died'. Others, too old to go to war, tried to keep going. Edward Bowden's school in Bedford limped on until 1917, when he ran out of pupils 'owing to war'. Henry Griffith had taught shorthand and book-keeping at Malvern College but 'senior boys who would have come to him joined the army'. Some could not cope with the pressure – Ernest Frederic Row had 'a nervous breakdown due to overwork during the war'.

One or two were simply situated in the wrong place. Henry Waymouth was Principal of a school in Broadstairs but found 'his income halved as a result of the war and loss of pupils caused by Air Raids and Bombardments'. George Fraser had been a Headmaster in Walmer, Kent since 1912, but was unable to continue 'on account

---

[*]   M.E. Ruf(f) was appointed Instructor in French at the Royal Military College on 17 September 1903. In the College's First World War Roll of Honour, under the heading 'Officers on the Staff of the RMC', there is an entry for Captaine E. Ruff, L'Armée Francaise.

MEADOWFIELD HALL SCHOOL.

WHITBY.

DAY AND BOARDING SCHOOL FOR BOYS.

Provides a Sound Education for All Branches of Business or Professions.

Careful, Practical, and Individual Teaching. A model School fo requipment, accommodation, and results.

GAMES. GYMNASIUM. DRILL.

PREPARATORY DEPARTMENT FOR LITTLE BOYS, 5-7 years of age.

Next Term commences on January 18th, 1915, at 2-30 p.m. New pupils admitted at 9-30 a.m

Prospectus on application to the Headmaster.

D. CURRIE, B.A.

48   *Meadowfield Hall School's advertisement appeared the day the German shells hit.*

of [the school's] position and the air raids. His partner was in the Services and badly wounded.' Fraser wanted to move his school to a safer location but the Society refused to help as the 'Committee felt unable to extricate him from his difficulties.' Francis Davison Currie, Principal of Meadowfield Hall School in Whitby, saw 'half the [school] destroyed during the raid on Scarborough and Whitby' in December 1914.[*] The National Relief Fund sent him to the Society. Arthur Southee was referred by the same organisation. His problems had started well before the war: in 1903 he had sold his school, which he had begun and run in Ramsgate for 39 years, in order to look after his wife, 'who was in delicate health'. Unfortunately his successor had not paid him for the school (West Cliff) and he was ruined as a result. Since then he had earned a 'precarious living teaching foreigners. The War put an end to this.'

And there were other sorts of tragedy. Major Harold Arthur Denham DSO, a Cambridge-educated headmaster, was a member of 'the Territorial Army and mobilised in 1914. Served in France. He was twice wounded and mentioned in despatches. Shot himself in July 1921.' Mrs Catherine Steele's husband had been head of a Preparatory school in Walmer; he 'served in the army as a private and later as an officer … committed suicide in her presence'.

For all the sadness caused by poverty or war, there are occasional glimpses of hope which must have heartened the Committee in their work. Letters of gratitude from recipients were not usually preserved, but on 28 October 1882 the Committee recorded one from 'a SS Jones who was assisted by the Society in qualifying himself for the Bengal Civil Service in which he now holds an appointment. [He has] sent the Secretary £21 for the purpose of qualifying for the Society four of his old masters'. He wished his donation to remain anonymous, and so it did. The four accepted gratefully. Another letter which appeared to pose a problem, in the end did not. Mrs Edmonds of Bishopton had recommended Henry Rose to the Society. He had been an usher in her father's school and for 11 years the Society had made a grant of £12. She now wrote, indignantly, that 'the old man had imposed on the Society as well as her family and others; and that, so far from requiring help, he had regularly invested the grants voted to him for the benefit of his nieces'. In its great wisdom the Committee decided to do nothing.

---

[*]   On Friday 18 December 1914, when the bombardment began, the school was at morning prayers with the headmaster, Currie, praying 'for deliverance from our enemies'. The bombs then hit. On the same day, the *Whitby Gazette* carried an advertisement for pupils for the school. Nobody was injured in the attack, and the school limped on until May 1916.

11

Tales of Distress and Dishonesty

By no means all applications were, or are, successful. A few are rejected for technical reasons, but over the years some people have sought to obtain money from the Society by dishonest means. Most charities, aware of such people, share their information. Yet, despite vetting and investigation as thorough as the times allowed, some did slip through the net. As might be expected, these were often very sad cases.

Edward Pizzey was a 39-year-old usher in the London area. He was married to Emily, who was charged in 1866 with begging in Kensington. They had lived at 114 London Wall for about three months and *The Times* (*see* page 65) reported that when Inspector Jackson went there he

> found no furniture, neither chair, table nor bed. The Prisoner and her husband slept on the floor … they had not had any food for three days … the husband was a man of good education, and could speak several languages … he hoped to recover his position and had parted with everything and paid for advertisements for situations, when his children wanted food. He was educated for the Church.[1]

The magistrates remanded Emily and called for more information. We do not know the outcome but it is unlikely to have been favourable to the Pizzeys for the Society, which had supported Edward on three previous occasions, did not do so again.

Claiming money by false pretences was not uncommon. John Frederick Scott was another usher, who lived in Drury Lane. He claimed to have taught in Exeter, but on enquiry it was discovered that the school concerned had no knowledge of any Scott teaching there at any time. William James Smith, aged 33 and married, had neither position nor money when he applied to the Society, having previously approached the Charity Organisation Society. He claimed in a long letter written from the Infirmary, City of London Union on 1 October 1895, to have degrees from Cambridge and London, and to be going blind and thus unable to teach; instead he was hoping to start up as a newsagent and stationer. Unfortunately for Smith, COS's investigation revealed that he was not as well qualified as he claimed, and that proceedings were being taken against him in order 'to recover money gained by false pretences from a lady to whom he represented himself as unmarried'. None of his referees really knew him and none said anything in his favour.

Cases such as this show the advantage of co-operation between charities and the value of careful investigation by COS. But not all cases needed too much vetting: Robert Conboy Lifford of County Donegal applied in 1886 on the grounds that he had become an orphan at the age of 40 – he didn't win support. Nor did David Chapman of Sevenoaks, who was 69 when he came to the Society's notice. He was supported by several referees, including Earl Stanhope and Lord Sackville. After teaching in England he had gone to Australia but had been ruined by Australian Bank failures and forced to return to this country. He had been rescued from the Union in Sevenoaks when, unwisely as it turned out, he approached the Revd Dr William Baker, Headmaster of Merchant Taylors' School, Prebendary of St Paul's Cathedral, and, of most significance in this case, Treasurer of the Society. Baker sent him away. Chapman, nevertheless, wrote to the Head:

> Reverend Sir,
>   I called on you this morning expecting to meet a Christian gentleman. I am very sorry I made such a mistake. I might have known better from the deportment of your officials.[2]

Baker circulated other societies and headmasters:

> If a Mr David Chapman representing himself to be a distressed schoolmaster should call upon you, he is not a man to be encouraged.[3]

The Society did not always get it right. In 1882 John Abercrombie Leslie applied for, and was given, support from the Society, a compound leg fracture having curtailed his teaching career. However, in 1891 he was up before the Wandsworth bench, having stolen an umbrella belonging to the Revd Donald Matheson of Putney Presbyterian Church, which he then tried to conceal in his trousers. When charged, Leslie was also found to be in possession of letters containing remittances from the Duke of Fife and the Earl of Aberdeen. He was another who had sought to get money from Dr Baker. Leslie got no further help from him or the Society; instead he got three months' hard labour. *The Times*, in reporting the case, noted that Leslie had 'been in the habit of writing letters to the nobility, enclosing the copy of a letter purporting to have been written by the Society of Schoolmasters, Adelphi Terrace, recommending him for their consideration and support'.[4]

Bruno von Hohnfeldt was known to most charities between 1890 and 1903. He also answered to the names Arthur Cecil Temple and Thomas Olver Harding – the latter being someone who had actually died in 1876. Von Hohnfeldt was a well-educated German who approached the Society for Organising Charitable Relief and Repressing Mendicity in 1890 for help, which was given to him. He got a job in Eastbourne, but was sacked after two months for drunkenness. As he left he stole a coat belonging to the Headmaster, and went on to forge letters and steal from the till of a public house. He was charged with obtaining money by false pretences and theft,

At WANDSWORTH, JOHN LESLIE, an elderly man of clerical appearance, was charged with stealing an umbrella belonging to the Rev. Donald Matheson, minister of the Putney Presbyterian Church, residing at 13, Dealtry-road. The prosecutor stated that on Tuesday afternoon the prisoner called at his house and asked for clothing to enable him to accept a teaching engagement. Witness was unable to provide the prisoner with clothing, but he gave him food. After prisoner had left witness missed the umbrella from a stand in the hall. He followed the prisoner, who denied having taken the umbrella. Witness insisted on the prisoner's unbuttoning his coat, and he then admitted having the umbrella, which was partly concealed in his trousers. Witness at first hesitated to charge the prisoner because he appeared to be a man of education in difficulties. From papers which were found upon him the police thought that he was a begging impostor. Witness then charged him. Detective Cooper mentioned that the prisoner appeared to have been in the habit of writing letters to the nobility, enclosing the copy of a letter purporting to have been written by the Society of Schoolmasters, Adelphi-terrace, recommending him to their consideration and support. Upon the prisoner were found letters from the Duke of Fife and the Earl of Aberdeen, and Mr. Richard Chamberlain, M.P., those from the two noblemen having contained remittances. Mr. Chamberlain stated in his letter that he would jeopardize his seat if he gave pecuniary assistance to individuals in the constituency which he represented in Parliament. The officer added that the prisoner had given an address at 92, Westminster-bridge-road, which was a common lodging-house. Prisoner.—May I interrupt? I did not give that as an address, but as a place where I lived one night. Detective Cooper also stated that a number of pawn-tickets were found upon the prisoner. Mr. Denman granted a remand for inquiry. *Should be 'to'

49 *All cases are sad, though some have their amusing side as John Leslie's demonstrates: The Times, 3 December 1891.*

50 *William Baker, Headmaster of Merchant Taylors' and Treasurer to the Society.*

and in April 1892 came up before the Lord Mayor, who committed him for trial. In his defence, von Hohnfeldt said that he had been suffering intensely from neuralgia and had been drinking and taking opium to relieve the pain, and that he had suffered a mental aberration when he committed the crime. He got 12 months' hard labour.[5] By 1893 von Hohnfeldt had become Arthur Cecil Temple, claiming to be a graduate of Trinity College, Dublin, and a PhD of Heidelberg. He was associated at this point with a disreputable barrister who was also writing begging letters. Von Hohnfeldt was convicted as Arthur Temple.

Undeterred, in 1894 he was appealing from the Chelsea Workhouse, in the name of Dr Holmfield, for help to go to a convalescent home. This time he claimed to be a graduate in Mathematical Honours of London University and to hold a PhD from Dublin. In 1895 he was sentenced at the Central Criminal Court to three years' hard labour for obtaining money by false pretences from Sir Leopold M'Clintock and forgery. The police, who by now were getting to know him quite well, stated that von Hohnfeldt had connections with a gang of men who obtained money from clergymen by writing begging letters, sometimes on the paper of the Inner Temple Reading Room.[6]

Merchant Taylors' School.
E.C.

October 23. 1896

Dear Mr Roberts

I have had a letter from a
Clergyman in S. John's Wood
asking what I can tell him about
a Mr a Dr Leslie who has
been begging of him and making
use of my name as having
helped him on a previous occasion
My recollection is that

he is a man whom we
helped on one occasion, &
afterwards found out to
be a very undeserving
character, & I rather
think that he has
appeared at the Police
courts in connection with
his disappearance of

51   Letter, written in 1896, by William Baker, Headmaster of Merchant Taylors' School, to the Secretary of COS seeking information about John Leslie.

whichever poor houses he
has visited.

Some few years ago I
had a similar letter to
hand I have just received
from a Clergyman in
Hampstead about (I believe)
his same man —
My memory is however
rather bad for names
& I want to be quite
sure that I am correct

in his case
both you kindly give me any
particulars you may have
in your possession about Mr
(or Dr) Leslie. Does not the
C.O.S. know something about
him? He has evidently
got some old letter of mine
& is making use of it.

I am,
yours very sincerely
William Baker

A. L. Roberts Esq

52 *Bruno von Hohnfeldt
attracted widespread attention:* The
Times, 5 October 1895.

At GUILDHALL, BRUNO VON HOHNFELDT, 41, a tutor, was finally examined before Mr. Alderman Faudel Phillips on the charge of forging an endorsement to a cheque for £7 and uttering the same with intent to defraud. Admiral Sir F. L. M'Clintock, K.C.B., on August 29 received a letter in which the writer stated that he was in temporary difficulty and asked for assistance to enable him to return to his regiment. The letter was signed " Algernon T. W. Skeffington." The Admiral, having some knowledge of Skeffington and believing the letter came from him, sent £7. A few days after he received a wire purporting to come from Skeffington asking for £5 further. He was at Ryde at the time, and placed the matter in the hands of the police. Thomas William Clarke, financial agent, stated that he knew the prisoner as " the Baron." On Saturday evening, August 31, he saw him in the Cheshire Cheese, Fleet-street. The prisoner had a cheque for £7, which he said he had received for literary work. Witness got the waiter, Coles, to lend £1 on it, asking him to get the cheque passed through as quickly as possible. On the following Monday Coles advanced another 10s. On Tuesday the clerk to the proprietor of the house told him the cheque had passed through and handed him the balance, less £1 12s. 6d. and 2s. 6d. for clearing. Witness gave prisoner £5 5s., and the latter handed him 5s. for his trouble. It was shown that the prisoner had received letters at 14, Cursitor-street in the name of Skeffington. One was identified as coming from the prosecutor. Detective-Sergeant Bryan said the prisoner had been convicted for obtaining money by false pretences and burglary. The Alderman committed him for trial.

This did not stop him either, though, and in 1898 he got a further six months' hard labour for 'trying to gain a dishonest livelihood',* having failed to report in accordance with the terms of his licence. In 1899 he was 'impersonating a deceased Senior Wrangler, and is evidently an incorrigible rogue',[7] as the Secretary of the Society for Organising Charitable Relief and Repressing Mendicity wrote.† The following day C.S. Loch, the brilliant Secretary of the Charity Organisation Society, wrote to the Society to report that von Hohnfeldt was in Rustington Convalescent Home, Littlehampton, where he said that he had been given permission to stay for a further month by the founder of the home, Sir Henry Harben. 'We wrote to Sir Henry,' disclosed C.S. Loch, 'and, I think, have probably put a spoke in Bruno's wheel.'[8] This correspondence shows the level of co-operation between charities, for it was occasioned by the Society of Schoolmasters enquiring about one Thomas Olver Harding who was claiming distress as a result of 'surgical operations at St Thomas's Hospital, followed by a stay in another convalescent home'. Harding was 'really our old friend Bruno von Hohnfeldt', wrote COS.[9]

---

*   Florence Nightingale wrote in the 1880s that, 'Labour should be made to pay, better than thieving. At present it pays worse.'
†   The Society for Organising Charitable Relief and Repressing Mendicity operated from the same address as COS and the two were in effect the same organisation.

Enc.   C. S. LOCH, Sec.,   Charity Organisation Society,
          to whom all communications should
          be addressed.   15 BUCKINGHAM STREET, ADELPHI, W.C.

Telegrams—"ORGANISATION, LONDON."
Telephone—35,529 (Gerrard).
Office Hours—10 to 4. Sat. 10 to 1.
                                                                  Nov. 2nd. '99 189

    Private & Confidential.

    15659.

    Dear Sir,

            Thomas Olver(not Overend as you have it) Harding is really our

    old friend Bruno Von Hohenfeldt.   I enclose you a copy of a report which

    we have lately sent to several inquirers.   Hohenfeldt is at the present

    time is at the Rustington Convalescent Home, Littlehampton, where, he

    said in a recent appeal, he had been given permission to stay another

    month, by Sir Henry Harben, who is the founder.   We wrote to Sir Henry

    Harben, and I think, have probably put a spoke in Bruno's wheel.
                                            I am, yours truly,
    A. Llewellyn Roberts Esq.
          7, Adelphi Terrace, W.C.   Loch.

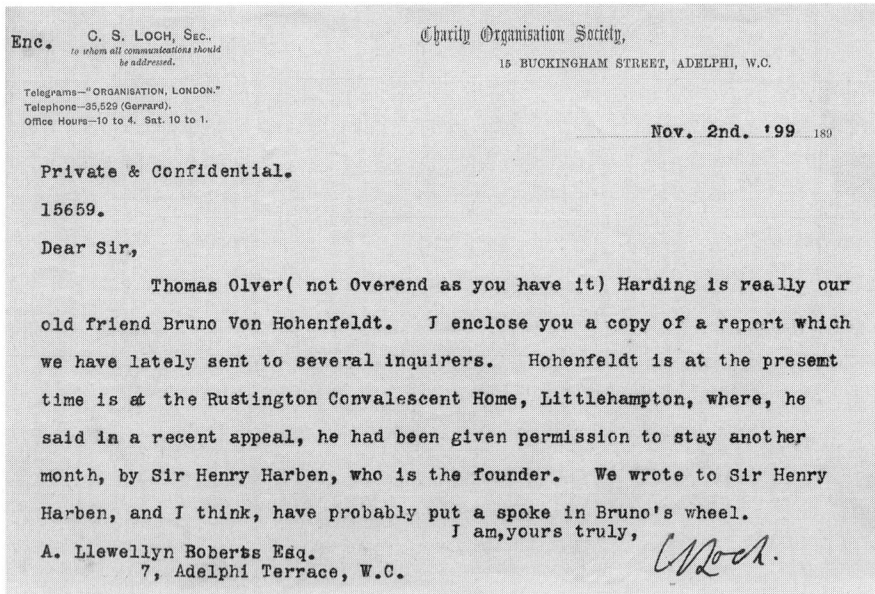

53   *C.S. Loch, the widely admired Secretary of the Charity Organisations Society, writing about von Hohnfeldt. The sharing of information was important to all charities.*

Von Hohnfeldt was only 39 when he applied to the Society in 1899 but he was 53 when he came up at Bow Street, four years later, this time in the company of a 38-year-old needlewoman. He was charged with being in the unlawful possession of letters. This time von Hohnfeldt claimed to be a doctor, writing on behalf of a nearly blind and poor 'patient' who had been at college with him. Described earlier by *The Times*, which reported all these cases, as 'an impudent impostor',[10] he was remanded for sentence. His real wife had gone back to her parents in Yorkshire years before.

Mrs Elizabeth Susannah Munns was 69 and a very different cup of tea. Her husband, William, had died in 1911, leaving his widow with £9 a year from investments and a government pension of 13s. 8d. a week, her son having died on active service. She applied in 1922, claiming that Mr Munns was already married when he married her. She doubted 'her own marriage was legal'. Unfortunately she could not remember too much about it, claiming it was solemnised at Camden Town but not knowing in which church, and that she was 35 when she married, having been engaged for 17 years.[11] The Committee was not convinced that the dates added up.

Attempts at fraud meant that vetting procedures had to be very tight and co-operation between charities close. Fraud did not go away because of this, but there was probably less of it on the grand scale. In 1922 Edwin Short had received £10 from the Society but six years later he was convicted for obtaining money under false pretences, and the Society gave him no more.[12] John Hayden Righton was also refused help 'because it was believed he was not out of employment, as stated by him'.[13] He tried again twice more, though on different grounds, on one occasion asking for help to pay for organ lessons. There were a few wishful thinkers: Harold Goodburn was

In August 1894, he again applied for his Railway fare to Eastbourne- this time appealing to a Clergyman in London by whom his case was refer- red to this Society. It was found that he was living in a Common lodging house, and he declined to again place his case in our hands.

The man has a wife and three children, all of whom live with, and are supported by, the wife's father in Yorkshire.

The Charity Organisation Society does not recommend any assistance being given.

ADDENDUM. JULY 1896.

In August 1893, Von Hohenfeldt was begging in the name of Arthur Cecil Temple, describing himself as a graduate of Trinity College, Dublin, and Ph.D. of Heidelberg. He was at that time associated with a disreputable barrister, who was also writing begging letters.

In 1894 Hohenfeldt was appealing from the Chelsea Workhouse in the name of Dr. Holmfield for help to go to a Convalescent Home. This time he represented himself to be a graduate in Mathematical Honours of the Lon- don University and Ph.D. of Dublin.

On the 21st. Oct. 1895 he was sentenced at the Central Criminal Court to three years hard labour for forging the endorsement to a cheque which he had obtained by representing himself to be another person. It was given in evidence that he had been previously convicted in 1893 in the name of Arthur Cecil Temple of obtaining money by false pretences.

He is now personating a deceased Senior Wrangler, and is evidently an incorrigible rogue.

ADDENDUM. JULY 13.1899.

On August 5 1898 Hohenfeldt was charged under the Prevention of Crimes Act with failing to report himself in accordance with the terms of his license. It was shewn that he had been endeavouring to gain a dishonest livelihood and he was sentenced to six months hard labour.

C S Lochfer

54 *Loch's initial letter to SOS's secretary, A.L. Roberts, about von Hohnfeldt.*

Report.] [Form No. 36.

SOCIETY FOR ORGANISING CHARITABLE RELIEF AND REPRESSING MENDICITY.
CENTRAL OFFICE : 15 BUCKINGHAM STREET, ADELPHI, W.C.

N.B.—This Report is CONFIDENTIALLY communicated, and intended only for the information of *A. Llewellyn Roberts. Esq*

Case No. 15659. Date of Report 1st. Nov.1894 Despatched *Nov 2nd 1894*
Name **Bruno Hohenfeldt, or Von Holmfeldt.**

Address

This man, a German of good education, and formerly a schoolmaster, first became known to this Society in May 1890, through his asking for help in money and clothes to enable him to get work as an Assistant Master in a school. In April 1891 he obtained a situation at Eastbourne, and the necessary clothes were provided. In June he was dismissed for drunkeness and was subsequently convicted of stealing a coat from the Head Master of the School where he had been engaged, but at the request of the Head Mas- ter was not punished. In the following August he applied to another branch of the Society, saying that he had just been engaged by a School- master at Eastbourne, and wanted his railway fare. He presented a letter from the Eastbourne Schoolmaster, and the money was advanced. That letter proved to be a forgery.

In April 1892 he pleaded guilty at the Old Bailey to two charges , one, of breaking and entering a public house and stealing money from the till, the other, of obtaining money by false pretences from the Pad- dington Committee of the Charity Organisation Society. He was sentenced to 12 months hard labour.

* Investigation often involves visits to several persons and a reference to the Committee of some other District, as well as communications by post with distant persons, who may delay their replies.

rejected because he already had a salary of £520, which in 1930 was not bad; Charles Henry Wisley was just incompetent: 'his annual outgoings [were] too considerable to be dealt with by the Society';[14] T.E. Thomas applied through his wife, but he wasn't on the staff of Sherborne as he claimed; in 1932 Captain George Anthony was turned down because he had 'ceased to be a schoolmaster in 1914 and was now a dealer in antiques'.[15] And sometimes applicants failed to do their homework: Alfred Rowberry Williams did not realise the Society shared the Secretary and premises of the Royal Literary Fund and Williams was turned down 'because he had left the profession and become an author. His application did not disclose that the Literary Fund had recently given him the help which he now asked the Society to provide.' The Secretary was only too happy to point this out![16]

12

Drifting Towards Crisis

In the years before 1914 the Society had got itself into a sound, though not wealthy, position. It had tightened its organisation and had a hard-working Committee backed by good local support. Things changed after the war, and not just because of it. The Society entered another period of drift in the late 1920s and 1930s, and the Second World War only compounded matters. By 1947, when R. McArthur took over as Chairman, things were moving towards crisis point – and they did not improve for some years to come. McArthur's initial observation was that the Society had been in 'a somewhat somnolent condition for some years', which was a kind way of putting it, and he questioned the continuing purpose of the organisation.

The reasons for the decline are not difficult to find. While the First World War clearly had a direct adverse impact, maintaining the organisation and structure of the Society, upon which the financial prosperity depended, was also very difficult thereafter. In the years before 1914 there had been regular, usually annual, donations from a number of schools and their staffs. Among the leading ones were Dame Allan's, Charterhouse, Cheltenham, Christ's Hospital, Clifton, Eton, Haileybury, Oundle, Rugby, Sir William Turner's and Winchester, and their generosity continued for a while after the war. A decline set in during the late 1920s and 1930s, however, and by 1946 the number of subscribing schools had fallen from 30 to five, and these produced a total subscription of just £56 – in 1914 the nine major subscribers alone had contributed over £114. This fall was due in part to a failure to maintain the network of Local Representatives, or Correspondents, as they were now called, after 1918. While the days of local committees had gone, 32 such Correspondents covered 24 areas in 1911, and among them was the celebrated Etonian Headmaster and hymn writer, the Revd Cyril Alington; there were still 30 in 1920, but by 1946 the number had fallen to nine and in that year Wellington College discontinued its subscription. This reduction led to the Society's helping fewer people. In its first 100 years it had made about 3,700 grants, distributing over £38,000; between 1900 and 1914 a further 553 claims were supported. In 1940, by contrast, the number of grants was 19, and in 1946 just fifteen.

The Society had always had a number of individual subscribers amongst its membership, and from time to time it received welcome and generous donations. In

55 *The links between the Society and Eton continue to be very strong. These three Eton Head Masters, Cyril Alington, Claude Elliott and Edward Lyttleton, did much for the Society.*

1867 Madame Tildesley de Bosset had made a bequest of £1,000 and in 1942 the former Treasurer, Charles Pendlebury, left an equal sum. The Society also received rather smaller amounts from well-wishers, as well as the collections from school chapel services and organisations such as the Conference of Schoolmasters and College Dons. The National Relief Fund gave money (£1,500 in 1920) to help meet cases of distress arising from the war. These sums, however, did not make up for the decline in monies sent in by subscribing schools, for it was from the money donated each year, together with the interest on investments (£471 in 1946), that grants were made.

The need to save money wherever possible was always present. In 1923 the Minutes noted that 'in dealing with all cases the Committee feels that the *increased* [my italics] purchasing power of money should be taken into account'.[1] However, a Rules revision the following year to include 'all schools other than Public Elementary Schools' within the Society meant that the need to maintain and increase funds was likely to be all the greater. In the 1920s and 1930s a weakening network of Local Correspondents managed to support Appeals made by the Committee, but these produced few new subscriptions – that of 1936 attracted three schools (Oakham, Charterhouse and Wellington). The poor response led the President, the Revd and Hon. E. Lyttleton, former Head Master of Eton, to suggest that subscribers should follow the Eton example and complete Deeds of Covenant, but little came of the idea.

The Officers of the Society changed too – and not just as a result of natural causes. In 1900 clergy still dominated the Committee – 12 out of the 16 were clerics – and the Presidents and Vice-Presidents were ordained to a man. Twenty-three local Chairmen were also men of the cloth. These were powerful men: in 1909 three bishops, two heads of Cambridge colleges, and the Provost of Eton were among the seven Honorary Presidents, and there were the heads of six major schools among the 12 Vice-Presidents. By 1920 things were different: there were only two Honorary Presidents and five Vice-Presidents, and the Chairman of the Committee was the only cleric on it. This reflects changing circumstances and may well have been a good thing; in itself it matters little, but a means of persuading reluctant donors was lost, and it was perhaps indicative of what was to follow.

This does not mean that the Society did nothing during the inter-war years. It continued to support cases and make grants as far as was possible. The Society continued to work very closely with other charities, in particular PCAC and COS. The dishonesty referred to was comparatively rare, but poverty and hardship were not. Many cases were similar to those of the last quarter of the 19th century, when there was a need to provide clothing and furniture so that men could take up positions, and PCAC appear to have been very good at this, whereas the Society was far better at providing teeth! D.B. D'Archy, already in the workhouse, was given £2 from petty cash in 1894 'to furnish him with the means to purchase some false teeth' and in 1929 Charles Blanchard got £5 for the same purpose. In 1935 the Committee discussed an enquiry from Douglas Best, aged 18, the son of a schoolmaster killed in the Great War, as to whether or not the Society might help him find a job.[2] While obviously outside the Committee's remit, the Minutes make no comment at all, a far cry from the days of 1800 – or indeed those of the 1880s – when more help would have been offered.

The Society was more sympathetic towards Bullen Spicer, whose name appears in the pages of the Society with almost monotonous regularity. Bullen Spicer, aged 57, had taught at Oundle but had been an undischarged bankrupt since 1908. His son by his first wife had fought in the First World War as a Lieutenant in the 6th Dragoon Guards and he had a two-and-a-half-year-old child and a baby of two months by his second wife when he originally applied. As they grew older Bullen Spicer, ignoring all rejections, persistently sought help for their (private) education and for clothing. In 1931 the Committee informed him 'that it was not disposed to further consider his case'. This didn't stop him or, after his death, his wife, from making applications, certainly until as late as 1952.

By 1939 the financial position had not improved at all and one application was turned down because 'the funds of the Society had been fully allocated for that year and it was impossible to help [the applicant]'.[3] Checks had been placed on spending in the past, but this was the first time such a response had been made.

The Second World War stretched the Society in more ways than just financial ones, though income continued to decline. For perfectly obvious reasons attendance at

Committee meetings and AGMs was difficult, and in October 1941 the Rule relating to a quorum was suspended for the duration of the war as only two or three members were able to attend. In December 1939 only the Treasurer, Pendlebury, and Secretary, Marshall, were present; they went ahead with the meeting and got their decisions confirmed at a later meeting in March 1940. With Britain in the grip of the 'Phoney War', but not under too much pressure, one wonders whether the poor attendance was on this occasion due to other reasons. The year 1943 saw a moment of high drama, for at the AGM the Secretary 'was authorised to open, by force if necessary, the iron box recently removed from the custody of Messrs Coutts [and now stored at Stationers' Hall] with the object of finding the Deed appointing the original Trustees of the Society'.[4] At the next AGM the Secretary 'reported that he had forced open the iron box and that its contents had been found to consist solely of very old receipts for grants made by the Committee in past years'.[5] These were destroyed.

It is difficult to ignore the feeling that the Committee was responsible for at least some of its difficulties in the inter-war years. The Chairman between 1926 and 1947, and a member since 1913, was the Headmaster of Owen's School, Islington, R.F. Cholmeley, and much respected though he was, the impression is that he did not offer much dynamic leadership; in consequence, the Society limped along.

It was during this period that the Society enjoyed one of its moves. It has had as many different venues as it has had Presidents and Chairmen,[6] but that is not as difficult as it might sound, given the length of time some remained in office. Following the *Crown and Anchor*, the Society had a long and fruitful association with the Literary Society, and when they moved so did the Society. The two charities shared a secretary and the Society paid a small rental charge for use of the premises. In 1921 this link came to an end when the College of Preceptors in Bloomsbury Square offered the Society a room free of charge, with a place in their strongroom for the all-important box. This offer was immediately accepted and so began an association with the College of Preceptors which lasted until 1948. Though the link with the College then came to an end, that with Bloomsbury did not, for the Society met at Owen's School from 1948 to 1953 and then at Gordon House, 29 Gordon Square, from 1954 to 1963.

During the early part of the 20th century Gordon Square was home to many of the Bloomsbury Group: the Bells, Vanessa, Clive and their children, lived at 46, an address to which Duncan Grant and Bunny Garnett came often; Lady Strachey lived at 51, and also resident in the Square were Lytton Strachey, Maynard Keynes and Raymond Mortimer. Virginia and Leonard Woolf lived in nearby Tavistock Square, the home of their Hogarth Press. Quentin Bell, one of Vanessa and Clive's children, recalls that he was taught by Miss Rose Paul, a classicist who taught boys Greek at Owen's School 'until there were no boys left learning the language. She continued to be connected to the school through its headmaster, Mr Cholmeley; the connection had I gather been romantic but was now so ancient as to be respectable'.[7] This was, as far as the Society is aware, the nearest it came to any scandal.

13

Crisis

The end of the Second World War in 1945 saw the Society in financial difficulties. The Committee's attempts to raise money were not helped by the assumption that the creation of a welfare state would end the need for such charities as SOS. Though the Society recovered almost £500 from the Inland Revenue for tax overpaid and unclaimed for four years this did little to improve matters, and in October 1946 a special meeting considered the position of the Society and its future policy. It decided to increase the size of the Committee so that it was more representative of 'at least the London schools', and also to allow greater flexibility over the dates of meetings. It agreed to discuss any Rule amendments at a future meeting. The enlarged Committee might eventually produce some fresh thinking, but the moves in themselves were unlikely to galvanise a moribund Society.

The new Chairman, R. McArthur, Headmaster of Parmiter's School, was only too well aware of the task that lay ahead and he spelled it out to the new Committee: the Society was somnolent and funds were low and getting lower. It had to decide whether it was to seek salvation by increasing its activities and subscribers or hand over its assets to another charitable institution. 'Grants,' McArthur added, indicating his own view, 'might not amount to very much but they did make a welcome difference between acute poverty and straitened circumstances.'[1] The Committee concluded that it should continue to help those who had no other organisation to call upon, and another Appeal was launched at the start of 1948, aimed at the heads of all independent and preparatory schools.

The Appeal did initially produce some response – £80 – but it also produced several questions about the purpose of the Society, some suggesting that the benevolent funds of larger institutions such as the National Union of Teachers and the Independent Association of Assistant Masters were doing much the same job. The Committee replied by sending a letter to schools which had not subscribed, answering these points and explaining the *raison d'être* of the Society.

While the Society welcomed any donation, subscription or bequest, its current account rarely topped £300, with a further £700 placed in the Post Office Savings Bank – and there were, of course, the invested assets. In 1948 the Society suffered a blow it could ill afford when the enforced transfer of its Railway Stock to the new

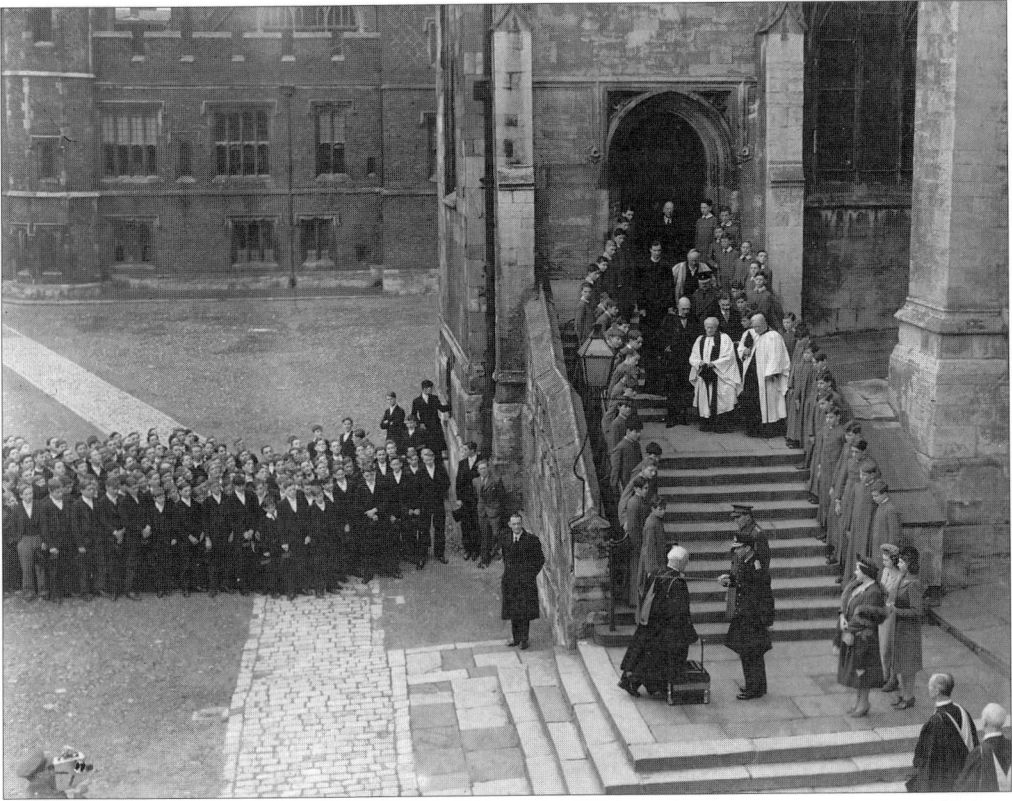

56   *Henry Marten was President during a very difficult time for the Society; here he is being knighted on the steps of Eton College Chapel in 1945.*

British Transport stock resulted in a loss of £25. It is one of the very few references to national events during this period.

Despite the Society's precarious position, G. A. Riding, retiring Head of Aldenham and a Committee member who had been keen to support the Appeal, resigned in 1949, having decided that the balance sheet 'presented so rosy a picture that he found himself unwilling to make any further appeal for support from his school', and he considered that the Society should spend at least £10,000 of its assets before asking for more subscriptions.[2] Perhaps he had eaten something which had disagreed with him! A suitable reply was penned by the Secretary and Chairman.

Much time continued to be spent on finance as the Society struggled to continue its grants. In 1950 the Treasurer reported that the Society had spent more than its available income and had raided the Post Office Savings account, a practice which was to continue. Coutts did all they could: in June 1950 the current account was down to £74, but a tax rebate of about £90 was expected and they agreed to honour cheques so as to avoid further withdrawals from the Post Office. This was generous but it did not hide the real problem, and the Society had to cash in some investments in order to cover any shortfall. Every opportunity was taken to reduce expenditure and the Secretary, C.B. Yule, suggested that the salary which went with his job (£100 per annum) was too much, given the Society's income. He retired and was replaced by Mrs Close at £60 per annum.

While the Post Office account continued to bail out the current account, McArthur was determined to keep the Society before the public eye and a booklet about it was distributed to all HMC and preparatory schools in an attempt to win more subscribers. The cost of printing, stationery and postage was £24 19s. 10½d. and there had been 'a disappointing response: £5 15s. 6d. in subscriptions and a seven year Covenant for £2'.[3] By October 1951 the Coutts Bank balance stood at £6 7s. 9d. and that of the Savings Bank at £502.

The Society continued to do its best for its cases, many of which have a familiar ring to them: Mr H.M.N. Reed asked for help to cover the 'rehabilitation of clothing'.[4] Others were a little more ambitious: Mrs B. Hindley, who was supported for many years, initially wanted to buy a house and the Society, keen to help, made her a grant of £26.[5] Some were turned down because they had too much capital: Mrs Druce had £2,000 and a house, and Mrs Whitestone 'a large amount of capital'. Mrs Banford's case showed how tricky things could be: she had failed to disclose a pension of £40 when she applied, and the Society had to rescind its grant as the National Assistance Board would stop their allowance of two shillings a week if Mrs Banford received any more money. Mrs Bullen Spicer continued to enter the lists: in 1950 she received a grant of £40 and the following year a grant was made conditional on the success of the school her two sons were running; she got another £40. In 1952 she applied for an old age pension, which she got, and the Society made her a final gift of £10. Even this did not stop her applying again within three months, but at last the Committee appears to have stood firm.

The Society helped a Mrs Montgomery, whose son was teaching in an unnamed independent school paying less than Burnham Scale, although it could not afford to do so. There were several similar cases. In March 1952 Mr H. Moore-Attwell was asked by the Committee 'if he had any suggestions to make regarding reducing the grant' made to him as he 'had received £325 since March 1949, which is a large proportion of our expendable income'.[6] There is a simple way by which the Committee might have reduced the grant, but it didn't take it and – almost inevitably – payments continued. The Committee's dilemma can be appreciated but some of these grants do seem like acts of folly. The payment made to Mr C. de Behr appears to have been an act of unwarranted generosity: de Behr could not produce a birth certificate to satisfy the Committee of his *bona fides* and refused to apply for an old age pension as he had been urged to do by the Society, but because he claimed 'his circumstances would be improved in the New Year' the Committee made him a final grant!.[7]

A year later the Savings Account was down to £145 2s. 2d., less than had been withdrawn from it during the previous year, and the Treasurer emphasised the need for the utmost economy in awarding grants. 1953 was to be a bad year: the Auditor, W.J. Langford, resigned; the decision was taken that 'no endeavour should be made to add to the number of Local Correspondents for the present'; and only McArthur, who never missed a meeting, and the Secretary arrived for the meeting of

57 *A.E. Conybeare, Vice-Provost of Eton, was President for three years.*

15 September 1953 and, as there was not a quorum for the first time in the Society's peacetime history, no meeting was held. At the AGM of 1954 the Chairman reported 'that the Society's income was now lower than perhaps it had ever been but means might yet be found to increase it ... and we ought to continue to administer our trust as before.'[8] He further pointed out that subscriptions were likely to continue to decline as most subscribers were elderly. It was decided to ask Coutts whether they would permit an overdraft 'for a few years' so that the many cases involving people over 80 could continue to be honoured. It did not prove necessary to pursue this.

The principal reason for this improvement might seem to confirm the power of prayer, though cynics will prefer to see it as merely a change of personnel. In April 1952 the President, A.E. Conybeare, had died and McArthur had written to the Provost of Eton expressing the regret of the Society and 'adding a prayer that the connection between Eton College and the Presidency should be continued.'[9] The Provost, C.A. Elliott, who would later be knighted, replied accepting the appointment of President and immediately got himself heavily involved, writing to schools and persuading the Eton staff to take out 13 deeds of covenant. McArthur reported that 1953 had been a very difficult year but, thanks to the President's efforts, the Society had avoided a deficit.

In his report, McArthur pointed out that subscriptions, the variable element in the Society's finances, had been badly affected by changes in social legislation during the post-war years, 'changes which have fostered the illusion that work such as ours is superfluous.'[10] It was a continuing theme of his annual reports. 'The welfare state has by no means met all the difficulties of schoolmasters and their dependants who fall by the way,' and 'There is a continuing need for our work, even now that the welfare state is popularly thought to have created Utopia,' are just two examples.[11] It is true that those helped tended to be the elderly and, not surprisingly, their numbers declined, but it is the case that, despite the State's efforts, there was a need for the Society among, in particular, former preparatory school masters and their families; teachers in senior schools invariably seem to have belonged to professional bodies which were able to look after their interests.

14

A Brief Respite

The work of Claude Elliott, especially at Eton, enabled the Society to meet its commitments and look towards the future. McArthur retired as Chairman in 1959, his period in office having coincided with one of the most difficult periods in the Society's history. His stewardship was one of resolute determination, for he was insistent that the Society should carry on helping a small but significant group of people. In his final report he drew attention to the help the Society had always received from Eton: successive Provosts and Head Masters had played prominent roles in the Society and encouraged their staff to contribute generously. There is a continuous link between the College and the Society in many different areas, some of which will be mentioned shortly. Besides the subscriptions raised from Eton, one benefactor deserves special mention: R.C. Martineau, from the 1950s, made a series of very generous donations, often at critical times.

McArthur was succeeded by C.R. Evers, who sought to widen the scope of the Society and win the support of more schools, as was the wont of new Chairmen. He sought, in particular, to bring in the preparatory schools, several of whose more elderly staff the Society was supporting. In this quest he was considerably aided by P.G. Mason, who was Chairman of the Joint Committee of HMC and IAPS and a Committee member of the Society. Evers was quite right to broaden the Society's appeal as much as possible, for the financial recovery was short-lived. The current account balance dropped rapidly in 1960 to £265 – a fall of £120 over the year – and the savings account continued to be raided and so plummeted from a precarious £130 in March to only £40 by November. The traditional Christmas gifts to grantees were not given in 1960, although small ones were reinstated the following year. At the AGM of 1961 it was reported that expenditure exceeded income by over £65. Attendance at Committee meetings also fell to four or five stalwarts. Yet again the Society had to retrench and, once more, Sir Claude Elliott led from the front, but after 10 years of very hard work on behalf of the Society he retired and was succeeded by R.J.S. Curtis, Public Relations Officer of IAPS, after the High Master of St Paul's, R. Gilkes, had turned the position down.

It would be wrong to assume that the Society's thinking during these years was totally dominated by finance, though obviously it played a part for it was an essential consideration if the primary objective of the Society were to be met. Case histories show the continuing need of an ageing, if smaller, group of people – in 1963 the Society made grants to 11 of these. The cases reflect the changing social conditions of the day, several receiving help from more than one source. D.P. Zumach was one man helped by the payment of his National Insurance contributions to ensure he received a pension on his retirement and death benefit as well. A widow with two young children was helped to help herself – an often unseen part of the Society's work has been the advice and comfort offered at times of real stress, and this personal aspect has been much valued. The Committee and its Secretary have always sought to keep in touch with those it has helped, either by visit or by letter.

While the Committee was anxious to ensure that its funds were not used to relieve public authorities of their responsibilities, it was just as keen to get accurate information about its applicants, for, as McArthur put it in 1959, 'the supply of impostors is not exhausted'. Several of those helped were widows, not all of whom were in receipt of old age pensions – one widow was helped 'because her husband's pension died with him and she was no longer eligible for any assistance from the State', such aid not coming until later. Most were in their 70s and 80s; typical was a widow of 87 whose husband had been a Headmaster and Inspector of Schools but had spent his last 33 years in a mental home. Two of their children lived in America and the third was a semi-invalid. The widow's total income was £195 and the Society's grant was limited to £14 per year, together with occasional gifts. Another 74-year-old had spent much of 1962 in hospital before moving to a Church of Scotland Home; the Society initially gave him £25 for badly needed clothing. Discovering he was allowed 10 shillings and sixpence a week for all his personal expenses – soap, razor blades, shoe repairs and the like – the Society made a grant of £52 a year. In the 1960s up to 13 applicants were helped and some £660 per annum distributed. Letters of appreciation showed how much this help meant, and nearly every applicant was visited by a headmaster living in the neighbourhood; the Committee found the resultant information very helpful in assessing claims.

By 1967 it appeared that far from declining, the need for the Society was increasing and the Committee therefore decided that an Appeal should be made to HMC and IAPS schools through their bulletins. After a very slow initial response, things picked up a little – HMC schools managed to raise £113 3s. and IAPS £78 12s. 6d. – but Evers described the Appeal as 'only a partial success', a euphemistic way of putting it. An attempt was made shortly after this to enlist the support of HMC and IAPS for greater publicity – again through their bulletins. While IAPS agreed to help, HMC did not; instead, they decided to give the collection from the annual Service of Compline to the Society. This amounted to 10s., rather less than the usual school chapel service! In a moment of generosity HMC made their donation up to £5. Again it was a very disappointing response.

During the economic and political uncertainty of the Wilson years – and then of the 1970s – the Society's portfolio received close attention. An investment in the Reed Paper Group had proved ill-judged, and other holdings were moved about regularly, including those of Charrington Breweries and Grand Metropolitan Hotels, both of which were sold. The Society had always kept a close eye on any legislation which might affect it and in 1969 Maurice Macmillan moved the National Insurance (Further Provisions) Bill in the Commons. It failed to get a second reading and, as a result, the wrong it sought to remedy remained, and 125,000 people whose average age was 86 still had no pension rights. It was the sixth time Parliament had refused to recognise the claims of those who could not be insured under the National Health Acts, and showed very clearly the need for charities such as the Society of Schoolmasters to remain in being.

Equally, it was necessary for the Society to keep its own Rules up to date and adjustments were now overdue – there had been none since 1950. The changes involved a protracted correspondence with the Charity Commission, which finally agreed an important clarification of those eligible for grants. This now included 'Masters of Primary, Secondary and Preparatory Schools', a significant change from 'Public Schools, Grammar Schools and Preparatory Schools'. Other changes meant that membership of the Society should now 'consist of all schools which made an annual subscription and all donors and subscribers to the Society's funds'. The reprinting of the Rules and booklet, even in pamphlet form turned out to be prohibitively expensive and so members were circulated with a typewritten version instead.[1]

From time to time, the affairs of the nation continued to impinge on the work of the Society, or at least its meetings. The AGM of 1971 had to be postponed from March to June 'because the postal strike had made it impossible to send out notices', and in 1974 the Auditors failed to complete the accounts in time for the AGM due to the 'national emergency' (the three-day week of Edward Heath's administration). During the 1970s the value of the Society's funds plummeted, and in 1975 it was reported that 'the market value of our holdings are about one half of cost; the last two years have been disastrous on the Stock Exchange, but the investments [are] sound'.[2] A similar report was made three years later, as Callaghan's 'winter of discontent' approached.

Despite what was going on in the country, the Society soldiered on. There were, of course, irritants, such as when the Secretary Mrs Close wrote to Evelyn King MP asking him to take up a case with either the Social or Welfare Services so that an applicant (a Mrs Eaton) might obtain Supplementary Benefit. King did not bother to reply, but the matter was settled satisfactorily without his help. Overall applications were few and larger bodies often combined with the Society to help those in need – an 88-year-old widow was helped by a combination of SOS, PCAC (itself not flush with money), and the Distressed Gentlefolks Aid Association (DGAA). This lady was young when compared with Mrs E.E. Fulford, who reached 100 on 22 July 1973, an event which was celebrated by gifts and flowers from the Society. Her husband had taught at King's College School, Wimbledon from 1902 to 1920, and she lived on her old age pension, a grant from the Musicians' Benevolent Fund and help from the Society; this enabled her to heat and light her damp basement flat until February 1973 when, aged 99 and no longer able to look after herself, she had to go into an old people's home.

The slender stream of applicants continued and the Chairman, writing in 1974, commented, 'As a pensioner myself now, I know how every little helps. There is no doubt that increasing prices, especially those of gas and electricity, are making things very difficult for our "necessitous" ex-colleagues and their families. I cannot see their needs decreasing yet.'[3] Certainly the Society did all it could to help ease people's last years. In 1973 it gave Mr C.L. Rotherham an extra £5 on top of his grant, writing to the Matron of his nursing home and asking her to help him purchase his cigarettes. He was 88, had a gangrenous foot and was almost blind, and was supported by the Officers Association, DGAA, PCAC, the Guild of Aid and the Society. Mrs Close, the Society's Secretary, managed to convince the Matron of the need and the Society sent Mr Rotherham 200 cigarettes each month, instead of a Christmas gift, until he died in 1975. It may not have been politically or medically correct, but it did probably ensure that an old man met his Maker with a smile on his face!

While help continued to be given for what might be regarded as the usual reasons – 'to buy clothing' (in 1976), debt, help in bringing up children – some needs had a more modern ring to them: electricity and telephone bills, lagging for leaking roofs, nursing home fees. For some, however, only advice could be offered: 'Mr Hilary-Smith was most unsettled and his wife did not like the new accommodation … [they were] advised to think well before changing again in view of their past difficulties.'[4] Others did not need help after all: 'Mrs Scott is thinking of moving and [does] not require the device to keep her central heating at a constant temperature.'[5]

The number of cases dealt with did not change much in the 1970s and 1980s and the reduction began in the following decade. Grants may not have been substantial – the maximum in the 1980s was £130 a year – but they did make a significant difference to those on a tight budget: 'We appreciated very much the Society's assistance of the past three years, as it enabled her to end her days in the home where she was so happy and well cared for,' wrote the niece of the widow of a grammar school master.[6] Such comments made it all worthwhile.

15

Salvation

Neither the beneficiaries nor the benefactors got any younger and in 1975, because of the likely reduction in income as generous donors died and were not replaced, a further Appeal was contemplated, aimed this time directly at staffrooms. The Chairman and President also pursued IAPS and HMC: the former sent a cheque and HMC managed the offertory (£85.50) from the annual service, which was a distinct improvement on their last collection. This all helped jog HMC into providing rather more support, if only for a time; IAPS continued to be responsive, spurred on by the President, R.J.S. Curtis, and P.B. Waterfield.

Evers was succeeded as Chairman in 1978 by J.L. Spencer and he, M.J. Shortland-Jones and P.B. Waterfield met at Eton to consider ways of increasing the income of the Society, as it was considered inadequate to serve the objectives. It was decided to seek contributions through personal approaches and to persuade HMC and IAPS actively to promote the Society through articles and letters in their relevant publications. They also recommended the use of Banker's Orders and Covenants – several years after they had been first mooted – chapel collections and school representatives actively encouraging annual contributions from their staff. It was a wide-ranging report[1] and, while it is easy to dismiss some of its suggestions as wishful thinking, many of its recommendations were in place and already working at Eton. Again Eton played its full part by printing the Appeal to Schools on its press, and Waterfield's school raised £82 through a collection. The IAPS Bulletin included a notice about the Society and its Assistant Secretary, M. Rawlins, was most supportive. The Chairman of HMC agreed to give 'sympathetic consideration' to the request for support but this was something the Society had heard before. None of it produced much in the way of immediate response, apart from a donation of £13 from Uppingham, and IAPS persuading the Greenrush Trust to contribute £125, and overall the Chairman, in his report of 1980, felt 'the drive had been a limited success'.

Finding money continued to be a major concern during the last quarter of the 20th century. A series of generous donations from livery companies (the Merchant Taylors', Skinners' and Wax Chandlers'), Trusts (the Martineau, Stanley Smith, Wightwick and Ludgate) and IAPS proved a considerable help. For a time HMC continued to donate the collections from its Annual Service of Compline, but its support had always been fickle and in 1995 it came to an end.

The Society could not rely solely on such sources, but many of its efforts to raise money in other ways in the 1970s and 1980s failed. An appeal was made to the Queen through the Keeper of the Privy Purse,[2] but this fell on stony ground – perhaps Her Majesty had looked up the previous correspondence! A further direct appeal to HMC Schools produced such a dismal response that the President concluded there was no point in extending it to other independent schools 'for the money spent on printing and postage could be better used.'[3] Articles about the work of the Society appeared in ISIS and *Conference* magazines but produced next to nothing. At one stage a professional fundraiser was consulted but any thoughts of using his services quickly disappeared as his charges would almost certainly have outstripped any receipts by a considerable margin. Nevertheless, the Treasurer could report in 1994 on 'a satisfactory situation but not an embarrassment of riches.'[4] It was too good to last, and in the following year John Davison was rather less sanguine: donations and investment income had fallen at the same time as the Society had decided to raise 'individual grants … in order to take advantage of altered tax hurdles.' He reported that 'we have been living beyond our means, and, therefore, it is essential to increase our funds or reduce our giving.'[5] In 1996 the Society had to sell some capital in order to meet commitments.

Certain measures of self-help, of which the Victorians would certainly have approved, did reduce overheads. An increasing amount of work was taken on by the Treasurer and Secretary; the services of Coutts, so long the Society's bankers, were dispensed with as they began to charge exorbitant fees for the privilege of acting as the Society's Custodian Trustees and little else. This responsibility was transferred, firstly to the Charity Commission and then to Capel-Cure-Myers, who did it all for little or nothing. The balance sheet was also improved by a fall in the number of beneficiaries. The number of recipients had always fluctuated and in the 1990s it varied between six and fourteen. Grants varied too: in 1992 nine beneficiaries received a total of £3,498. There remained no shortage of applicants though not all were eligible for help or were who they purported to be. A loan, fortunately small, made to a Mr Rees-Davies proved to be a less than wise investment as Mr Rees-Davies vanished with the proceeds and the loan had to be treated as a grant! Investigation into an application for help from a 19-year-old Ugandan lady, who claimed to be the daughter of a teacher who had died leaving 12 children, suggested the Society would be unwise to assist and it didn't.

Not all applicants sought long-term support, and the Society was able to help in a number of short-term cases, as it had always done: these included the father of a psychotic and suicidal son, and a person changing sex. For the most part, cases continued along familiar lines – telephone rental, chimney repairs, the redecoration of a room – though some were concerned with more specifically late 20th-century problems, such as help with computers or difficulties arising from credit card debt and loan sharks. There were still those needing help through lack of a pension, and those who were vulnerable – 'an honest but improvident man' was how one such was described in 1998.

The link between the Society and Eton is still strong. The staff has consistently supported the Society through subscriptions and collections and there have been several acts of great individual generosity, ranging from the munificence of Martineau, already alluded to, and more recently a bequest of £15,000 by the former Vice-Provost and long-time friend of the Society, Tim Card. But it has not always been through such direct means that the Society has benefited: the sale of the Eton Christmas cards, organised by Mark Phillips, who has designed and produced cards each year since 1985, has provided an income which has made the difference between

58, 59 & 60 *Benefactors such as R.C. Martineau and Tim Card have made wecome donations. Dick Curtis, of IAPS and the Society's President for several years, did much to foster links with preparatory schools.*

profit and loss on the Society's account. And as the Society has sought to increase its revenue, so Eton has played host at successful receptions for Chairmen and heads of schools. In the same way the King's School, Canterbury and Berkhamsted School have been most generous. It would be wrong, however, to assume that no other schools have played any part in the fortunes of the Society: Merchant Taylors' School and the Merchant Taylors' Company have had connections from the beginning and it is entirely appropriate that the current President, David Skipper, was Headmaster of that school, thus maintaining a link which goes back before Baker.

The Society has been served throughout its life by men, and more recently women, who have given many years' work to its furtherance. Among the several who fall into this group are its Secretaries and Treasurers. Arthur Llewelyn Roberts was Secretary to both the Society of Schoolmasters and the Royal Literary Society, and died in 1919. *The Times* obituary records that:

> he was educated at Eton and Magdalen and carried out the business [of the Societies] on a very small salary, single-handed, his heart being entirely in the work. London is plentifully provided with begging-letter writers and impostors … in dealing with them Roberts showed a masterly skill. As a rule they knew him too well to risk an interview with him. If they ventured to see him, he cross-examined them gently and patiently, and sooner or later made them perceive that they would do well to transfer their activities elsewhere. With those, on the other hand, who were genuinely the victims of misfortune, his delicacy and perseverance were boundless. He had the tact which perceives the nature of distress, and hastens to help, and yet not to wound, the sufferer.[6]

The same might have been said of Mrs Close, who served the Society for 33 years from 1951-84, of Mrs May Freeburn, wife of a master at Eton, whose knowledge of the applicants and Society were second to none, and of Mrs Brenda Skipper, wife of the present President. Amongst the Treasurers who have served the Society is Stanley Smith, who died in his nineties, having joined the Society in 1960; he scarcely missed a meeting before his retirement in 2003. To his wise judgment the Society owes a great deal: not everyone would force Coutts to admit a mistake – a letter about an investment had been sent to the wrong address – and then make them pay for their error.

In 1997 the Society celebrated its 200th Anniversary with a Eucharist in St Clement Danes in the Strand on 12 January. This was followed by a luncheon in the *Lyceum Tavern* which was as close to the long defunct *Crown and Anchor* as the Society could get. These events were 'reported on the Court Page of *The Times* and produced one donation, three requests for help and a lot of interest'.[7] This was very much in keeping with earlier traditions, as was the dinner held at Eton College to mark the agreement of a closer association with the Schoolmistresses and Governesses Benevolent Institution (SGBI).

It might be thought that small charities should amalgamate or, in the case of the Society, throw off its male exclusivity. Charity law does not make this an easy task, but it has not stopped the Society from seeking to do both. In 1997 it persuaded

61 & 62   *The architects of the links with SGBI, Keith Wilkinson and David Skipper.*

the Charity Commissioners to accept changes which allowed the inclusion of 'Schoolmistresses' within its title, and it also gave careful consideration to a possible amalgamation with another charity, something the Charity Commission was keen to encourage for it 'wanted small societies … to seek union with one another and merge' as this would increase their efficiency and effectiveness. As John Anderson, a Vice-President of the Society, had put it, 'while small may be beautiful, it is seldom practical'.[8] It was easier said than done, however, for union had to be between similar organisations, and when the Commission looked for a match of objects and needs, it found there were very few societies similar to SOS, even after the change to its more inclusive title in 1997.

A circular had been received from SGBI in 1982, and the then Committee of SOS had 'noted the existence of this organisation in case we were approached by someone who could be helped by it.'[9] Two years later SOS decided that it might be that 'someone' and R.W. Hayward came to explain the work of SGBI and to suggest that an interchange of Committee members might be of benefit. Thus began a lengthy period during which the two institutions nudged towards greater understanding. Progress was very slow, however, and it was not until 1993 that matters began to get really serious. On the surface there appeared no obvious impediment to an amalgamation, and by 2000 it was clear that the interest was mutual. Despite the very considerable difference in the assets of the two societies, the Society of Schoolmasters and Schoolmistresses would bring another dimension to the work of SGBI, whose Charter, amended by Act of Parliament in 1952, allowed it to help only schoolmistresses within the independent sector and not their dependants. SOSS had no such restrictions.

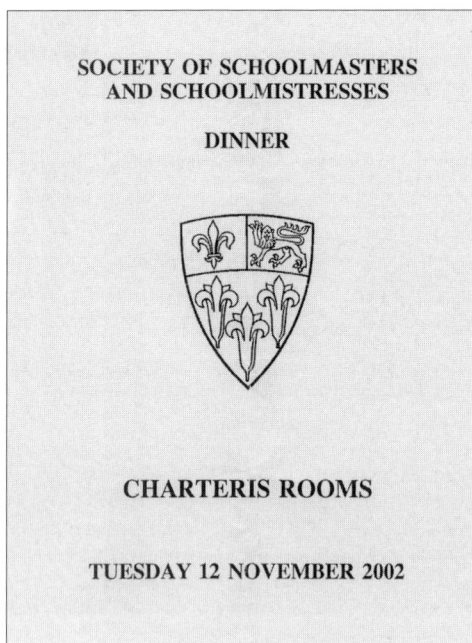

63   *Some things never change!*

Though a merger clearly made good sense, and the Chairman of SOSS and Headmaster of The King's School, Canterbury, Canon Keith Wilkinson, even declared at one point that 'nuptials are in the air',[10] the Charity Commission, tardy and obtuse to the last, thought otherwise and vetoed the idea. It ruled in 2002 that although both societies sought to provide financial assistance to retired school staff, the categories of people eligible for help by each society were incompatible and revision of the Trust Deeds was not feasible. Despite this setback, the two societies agreed a plan of co-operation by which the balances of SOSS were transferred to the SGBI bankers, who 'ring fenced' them in order to protect the interests of the male beneficiaries of SOSS; the plan also provided for common Trustees and administration. This new arrangement neatly side-stepped the Charity Commission, so keen for small societies to merge and yet, seemingly, less than anxious for such unions to take place. The two organisations clearly had much in common, even enjoying a Duke of Cambridge as their Patron, albeit different ones.

But it is those who benefit from the organisations that matter, and in 2002 the President of SOSS, David Skipper, wrote, 'Appeals for help [still] tell of genuine hardship and need. It is also clear that several of those who seek the Society's help require, first and foremost, professional advice and guidance so that they might be directed to the appropriate agencies and organisations. In this the Society has been pleased to be able to refer certain correspondents to the Case Worker employed by SGBI.'[11] That the Society continued to fulfil its objectives can be seen in the letters of appreciation it continued to receive. The daughter of a long-standing beneficiary wrote on her father's death, aged 92, how much SOSS meant to her as a child and to her brothers and sisters, who were able to say what they wanted for Christmas only when the Christmas cheque from SOSS arrived.

For about one hundred years, and certainly since Beveridge in 1942 and the arrival of the welfare state, successive Chairmen have predicted, sometimes gloomily, sometimes almost gleefully, that the State would never cater for all those in need. It would be easy to think that, as the Society's beneficiaries grow older and, with time, fewer, and as pension provision improves, certain charities will be made redundant. Our history suggests otherwise. Throughout the Society's existence its fortunes have fluctuated: there have been periods of considerable activity followed by periods of quiet consolidation and the odd one of crisis. Yet at no time has the Society failed to meet its commitments and there has never been a dearth of applicants.

SOSS has constantly adjusted its stance to meet changing conditions – it did so in the second half of the 19th century and again after the two world wars. More recently it has opened its doors to schoolmistresses and begun working in harmonious conjunction with SGBI. SOSS has often anticipated future needs and sought to make the changes necessary to meeting new challenges. Today the Society is continuing to provide vital aid and, as before, this has sometimes been given over long periods. It often makes the difference between a life of respect and one of pauperism. With the professional help of SGBI's case worker the help is perhaps better directed than at any stage in the Society's history.

Now in its third century, the Society is well aware that the need for it is likely to remain, sad indictment of our land though this may be. In some ways today's members are much like the Founders – headmasters and headmistresses meeting in common cause and dining, though less frequently. Heads have usually been one step ahead of the game, and it would be unwise to suggest that today's Committee is any less aware of the challenges that lie before it as it continues to fulfil the aims of those men who trudged down the Strand in 1797.

Appendix I
Further Information

Population of England and Wales

1801	8.7m
1812	10m
1830	12m
1841	15m
1861	20.1m
1871	22.7m
1911	36m
1951	43.8m
1981	48.5m

Average age of death in 1842

	Country	*Town*
Professions/gentry	45-50	34-44
Tradesmen/farmers	26-41	20-27
Labourers	16-18	15-19

Salaries/wages per annum

1800-25

1800	Rector/Vicar	£50 (and live well)
	Curate	£20
	A country gentleman	£3-400
	Head of a major school	Up to £1,000
	Labourer	£10-12
1810	Bishop of Durham	£19,066
	Bishop of Llandaff	£924
	3,998 livings were worth less than	£150
	1,061 livings were worth less than	£50
1815	Head gardener in a large house	£40 ⎫ these three would probably
	Experienced gardener	£26 ⎬ receive board and lodging.
	A butler	£50 ⎭
	Day labourer in garden	£15-20

1826-50

1826   Joseph Paxton got £70 per annum plus a cottage as a garden superintendent – this was not generous by the rates of the day. In 1838 he turned down £1,000 per annum to become royal gardener at Windsor. He left £180,000.

1830s   Earnings of over 30s. a week put a man at the top of the workforce.
A Durham miner averaged £1 4s. a week.
The Earl of Dudley had an income of £36,911 in 1833; by 1847 he had increased this to £157,900.

1840s   Staff at King Edward's, Birmingham (almost all ordained men) were paid £2-400 per annum, a figure which was doubled by capitation fees.
Witham National School, Essex, offered £55 per annum for a master and £35 for a mistress.
A tiny village school in Suffolk, started by the vicar, paid 10s. a week to the ex-farmer and his wife plus free housing and what they could collect from the children.
In 1845 the Prime Minister (Peel) earned £5,000 per annum.
In the same year the Viceroy of Dublin Castle (Clarendon) got £20,000 per annum and in 1848, at the height of the Irish Famine and European Revolutions, he spent £562 on butter and £1,297 on wine.
An Irish labourer earned 10d. a day.
A governess earned £25-30 per annum.
Hard cheese cost 2d. a pound.

1851-1900

1850s   Workers in iron mills could earn up to £3 a week.

1870s   A Highland crofter earned £8 per annum.
Agricultural labourers in Devon earned £18-21 per annum.
Adult workers in Bryant and May's Match Factory earned £28-33 per annum
In 1875 the Earl of Yarborough's cigars were sold for £850.

1900   A limekiln worker with six children in Bedfordshire earned 14s. a week.
Skilled artisans earned 30-40s. a week; a top footballer got the same.

RANDOM PRICES - THEATRE/ENTERTAINMENT/PRESS

1809   Covent Garden raised the price of seats in the pit (stalls) from 3s. 6d. to 4s., an action which led to violent protest.
Theatres were cheaper outside London – the gallery usually cost about 3d. – and remained so: in 1908 at the Theatre Royal, York, the gallery cost 4d., the upper circle 7d., and the pit 9d.

1840s   Lyceums began providing music, dancing, libraries and gymnastics at about 2s. a quarter.
A broadsheet newspaper cost 7d. (they had a readership of *c.*50,000)
A three-volume novel cost £1 11s. 6d. It is small wonder that Dickens, Trollope, Eliot, Thackeray and the like preferred the cheaper periodicals with their greater potential readership.
Membership of the Derby Town and County Library and Newspaper Room was £2 per annum, the Yorkshire Philosophical Society cost £5 on election and £1 per annum thereafter.
The cheapest single train ticket from London to Brighton in 1844 cost 4s. 2d. and from Leicester to Calais cost £1 11s.

Few of those helped by the Society of Schoolmasters or by other charities would have been able to afford the above.

A NUMBER OF DATES

1783	Britain recognises independence of USA.
	Pitt the Younger appointed Prime Minister.
1793	Britain declares war on France.
1795	Speenhamland System of poor relief begun.
1796	Jenner begins vaccination against smallpox.
1797	Economic crisis: Bank of England suspends cash payments. SOS founded. Burke dies.
1798	Malthus' *Essay on the Principles of Population*.
1799	Income Tax levied for the first time. Church Missionary Society founded.
1801	First full census. Pitt resigns and is succeeded by Addington.
1804	Pitt's second ministry.
1806	Pitt dies.
1811	Nash begins work on Regent Street. Luddite Riots begin.
1812	Widespread economic distress. Perceval (PM) murdered.
1814	Defeat of France. Edmund Keen makes his debut at Drury Lane.
1815	Waterloo and defeat of Napoleon. Davy's safety lamp. Nash begins Brighton Pavilion. Corn Laws passed.
1819	Peterloo Massacre. Six Acts passed to suppress radicalism.
1825	Stockton-Darlington Railway.
1828	Arnold appointed to Rugby. Repeal of Test and Corporation Acts gives religious liberty to dissenters.
1829	Roman Catholic Emancipation granted. Peel creates new London police force. *Rocket* wins competition for Liverpool-Manchester Railway.
1831	Charles Darwin sets sail in *Beagle*.
1832	First Reform Act.
1833	Slavery abolished in British territories. Oxford Movement's *Tracts for the Times*.
1834	Poor Law Amendment Act provides new structure for relief of poverty.
1837	First hansom cabs in London.
1838	Anti-Corn Law League founded. Chartism born.
1841	Newman's *Tract XC*.
1842	Chadwick's *Report on the Condition of the Poor*. Women and children prevented from working underground in mines.
1845-50	Irish Famine: 1 million die of starvation.
1846	Corn Laws repealed. Peel splits party and resigns.
1848	Year of Revolutions in Europe.
1849	Charles Kingsley and F.D. Maurice organise the Christian Socialist Movement.
1854-6	Crimean War.
1857	Indian Mutiny. *Tom Brown's Schooldays* published.
1859	*The Origin of Species* published.
1861	American Civil War starts.
1868	Gladstone's first ministry.
1869-70	Franco-Prussian War.
1870	Forster's Education Act.
1888	Keir Hardie founds Scottish Labour Party.
1889	Dock Strike.
1894	Local Government Act broadens relief for poor.
1895	Royal Commission on the Aged Poor.
1899-1902	Boer War.
1906	Liberal Government and reforms.

1908   First pension provided by State (5s. a week).

1911   National Insurance Act.

1914   Pensions to be given to the widows and orphans of those killed in the First World War.

1916   Unemployment Insurance extended.

1918   Fisher Education Act.

1919   Old Age Pensions Act raises basic pension to 10s. a week and remains at this level until the Second World War.

1922-39   Rising public expenditure and unemployment grows. Poor Law breaks down.

1922   Means testing introduced.

1926   General Strike.

1929   Poor Law Unions and Boards of Guardians ended. Wall Street Crash, Depression and economic crisis.

1934   Unemployment Act reduces benefit to 26 weeks.

1942   Beveridge Report.

1944   Butler Education Act.

1945   Family Allowance Act gives mothers 5s. for second and subsequent children.

1946   National Insurance Act.

1948   National Health Act. Poor Law abolished.

1952   Prescription charges introduced.

1966   Rating Act gives rate rebates to those on lowest incomes.

1971   Family Income Supplement introduced.

Appendix II
Biographical Notes

George Isaac Huntingford (**1748-1832**), who was Bishop of Gloucester and later of Hereford, was the Society's first President. He was a typical 18th- or early 19th-century prelate and, rather unusually, was criticised at the time for neglecting his diocese. Like many of his contemporaries he spent only the summer months there, but even when present he paid little attention to his duties, preferring the social whirl and good things in life.

Huntingford was the son of a dancing master and known as 'Tiptoe' when a boy at Winchester. He completed his education at New College, Oxford. A classicist, like so many, he wrote a textbook that became the standard work at Winchester for many years. The younger Charles Burney, however, thought little of Huntingford's Greek and slated his later *Monostrophics* in the *Monthly Review*. Despite this humiliation the two men remained friends.

In 1789 Huntingford was elected Warden of Winchester College and entered Wykehamist legend as a man of little imagination but great severity. He suffered a great deal of criticism which today might look a little unfair. Nevertheless, he faced two pupil uprisings. That of 1793 was put down when Huntingford threatened to bring in the militia and resulted in the expulsion of 35 pupils. The rising of 1818 was put down by troops with bayonets after Huntingford had asked his great friend Sidmouth (Addington) for help. Pupils felt let down as, they argued, Huntingford had hinted at reforms that were not forthcoming; they saw him as 'a lickspittle to the great and a bully to the young, a pedant, a liar and a cheat' (Frith). While there is no suggestion of impropriety, Huntingford's friendship with Addington, whom he had tutored, attracted criticism and he was regarded as 'politically not a wholesome influence'.

Huntingford's period as President coincided with the well-attended dinners to which royalty and, possibly, Addington came. His contribution to the Society was not ungenerous either in financial terms or in the efforts he made to help indigenous schoolmasters.

Samuel Goodenough (**1743-1827**) was Bishop of Carlisle and the next President. In some ways he was not dissimilar to Huntingford – he enjoyed good wine and treated illness with port and brandy – but there was more to him then that. Educated at Westminster, he went back to teach there before setting up a very successful school in Ealing for 'the sons of the nobility and gentlemen of position'. Though a classicist by training his chief love was botany, and he played a leading part in the Linnean Society, which had been founded in 1788.

His diocese needed careful handling and Goodenough demonstrated the necessary moderation, wit and elegance. Like Huntingford he spent only the summer months in Carlisle but, unlike him, he worked very hard during the four to six months he was there – even if his temper with drunken wagon drivers and clumsy servants was famously short. In Carlisle he wrote a cookery book and 'Bishop Goodenough's Pudding' remains a popular recipe.

Even though it took six days to travel from Carlisle to London, Goodenough was always willing to make the journey, taking with him his three wigs named 'Highty' (for London and state occasions), 'Tighty' (for official appearances in Carlisle) and 'Scrub' (for wearing at home). In his later years gout gave him a good deal of pain and restricted his attendance at SOS meetings.

The Revd William Barrow (1753-1836), the first Chairman and author of the original Address, was educated at Sedbergh and Queen's College, Oxford. He became Master of an academy in Soho Square between 1782 and 1799, the year in which he delivered the Bampton Lectures in Oxford. Though his interest in and work for the Society continued, he resigned the Chairmanship early in its life when he moved out of London. He was made Prebendary of Southwell in 1814 and in 1821 its Vicar-General. He ended his days as Archdeacon of Nottingham, to which position he had been appointed in 1830.

The Revd Dr Charles Burney (1757-1817), the brother of Fanny Burney, was educated at Charterhouse and Caius, Cambridge, where he enjoyed the pleasures of life. His gambling debts led him to remove 35 books from the University Library to a dark corner of his rooms from whence he tried to sell them in London in order to satisfy his creditors. Discovered, he was sent down in disgrace. Despite Fanny Burney's attempts to excuse her brother later, the disgrace hit the family hard and his father, the distinguished musicologist and historian, considered disowning him and forcing him to change his name.

Charles Burney then went to Aberdeen to continue his studies as well as his profligate life. Despite his lifestyle he established himself as a very considerable classical scholar and went on to publish several translations, pamphlets and books. As he sought to restore his reputation he taught for a time at Highgate School, before becoming the Headmaster of Dr William Rose's School in Hammersmith having married Rose's daughter. He later moved the school to Greenwich. Burney was well known for his strict discipline which, perhaps, accounts for the Revd William Jones' remarks referred to earlier (p.13). His road back to acceptance by family and society led to membership of the Royal Society, ordination, and appointment as Professor of Ancient Literature at the Royal Academy. When Matthew Raine had become Headmaster of Charterhouse in 1791, Burney had been one of his rivals for the position.

Burney retained his interest in the theatre from his youth, and in addition to a magnificent library had a fine collection of playbills, cuttings and newspapers. The British Museum was to buy this extensive library following his death with the help of a government grant of £13,500. A friend of Sheridan and Garrick, Burney was a wealthy man and he continued to live in style, enjoying his fine cellar until his death. In 1813 he handed over the school at Greenwich to his son, Charles Parr Burney, who like his father gave the Society devoted and generous, if a little less riotous, service. Charles Burney's bust is in Westminster Abbey.

The Revd Dr Matthew Raine (1760-1811) was educated at Charterhouse and Trinity College, Cambridge, where he was 16th Wrangler and a prize man before being elected a Fellow of his College. In 1791 he was appointed Headmaster of Charterhouse, where he enjoyed considerable success. A sympathetic man, though no soft touch, his greatest achievement was to improve the lot of the pupils by providing a single bed for each of them. In 1803 he was made a Fellow of the Royal Society. He was extremely generous to SOS.

The Revd John Hewlett (1762-1844) was Headmaster of a school at Shackleford in Surrey for a time after coming down from Magdalene College, Cambridge. He was to sell the school in 1802. Hewlett was a leading Biblical scholar of the day and was at one stage Professor of Belles-Lettres at the Royal Institution of Great Britain.

Dr Patrick Kelly (?1755-1842). Nothing is known of his parentage, early life or education before he became the Master of Finsbury Square Academy in London, a finishing school teaching commercial and mathematical subjects. Amongst its several buildings was an observatory.

Kelly was a mathematician and astronomer in his own right but his principal expertise lay in rates of exchange of currencies and in weights and measures, about which he wrote extensively. He was regarded as the leading authority in the country on these matters. English merchants lacked a reliable guide to exchange rates until Kelly drew one up, something the Bank of England had refused to do, though they were happy to accept Kelly's work after it appeared. Kelly continued to seek a wider guide to European rates but was continually hampered by the French and Napoleonic Wars. He also did work for the East India Company. Kelly was a friend of the leading scientists of the day, including Maskelyne, Herschel, Vince, Hutton and Raine, and his views were sought and respected by both Houses on matters of currency and exchange. His work on behalf of the Society was immense and, with his national reputation, it took a brave man to challenge his view. In the circumstances it is small wonder that the Committee came to rely on his advice and the Society was so reluctant to dispense with his services.

The *Crown and Anchor* tavern was in Arundel Street. A passage led from the Strand to the tavern and a further passage led to the church of St Clement Danes (St Clement was cast into the sea with an anchor around his neck). The land was once Crown property. The tavern was opened in 1726 on what is now No.37 Arundel Street but was pulled down and rebuilt in 1790, with one room for meetings measuring 84 feet by 35 feet. It was claimed it would hold up to 2,500 people and was the haunt of the intelligentsia, housing Hogarth's portrait of the Pretender, his wife and children. It ceased trading as a tavern in 1847.

Appendix III
Royal Correspondence

Sir William Knighton to the Revd Dr Russell:

Carlton Palace
Augt 7 1826

Sir,
I have had the Honor of approaching the King on the subject of the charity for the relief of distressed Schoolmasters.

His Majesty has been graciously pleased to command me to transmit annually the sum of fifty guineas, in aid of the funds of this Charity.

I have the Honor to be,
> Sir,
> > Your Sincere & faithful servant,
> > > W Knighton

On the death of George IV in 1830, a request that William IV continue the grant was made. Colonel Wheatley replied on behalf of the King:

Sir,
Your letter of July 7 requesting that his Majesty would be graciously pleased to continue the Subscription of fifty guineas towards supporting the Society of Schoolmasters which was granted by his late Majesty, has been submitted to the King and I am honoured by his Majesty's commands to inform you in reply, that his Majesty has been pleased to signify his intention of continuing the same support to that Society which it enjoyed during the reign of his late Majesty,
> Sir,
> > Your obedient Servt
> > > Henry Wheatley

St James Palace
July 28 1830

In 1844 Russell corresponded with Louis Philippe, now King of the French:

> Rectory House, Devonshire Square,
> Oct 7 1844

Sir,

   I take courage as Treasurer of the Schoolmasters' Society, which has the distinguished honour of claiming His Majesty, the King of the French, as an enrolled Member, to request you most respectfully to lay before His Majesty the accompanying statement of its funds.

   His Majesty will, perhaps, have some recollection of a dinner in the year 1816, given in celebration of the Birth-day of HRH the Duke of Kent, our Queen's illustrious Father, by the Societies over whose meetings His Royal Highness had at different times presided.

   I, at least, cannot forget how the King of the French on that occasion graciously condescended to converse with Dr Kelly, then Treasurer of the Schoolmasters' Society, and myself, Chairman of the Committee, and then Headmaster of Charter-house School, and recounted to us himself how he had been appointed a Teacher, and was pleased spontaneously to express his strong sense of the utility of our Society, and the blessing which it could not fail to prove to the indigent and unfortunate of the laborious and honourable profession to which His Majesty had himself belonged.

   His Majesty soon after sent Donations to the Society, and in a letter written under his own hand, conveyed warm expressions of sympathy with distressed Schoolmasters, and renewed commendation of the Society.

   It may not be unpleasing to His Majesty to know that the Society continues its good works, and still ministers relief so far as its limited funds enable it. Should an opportunity offer at which I might without presumption testify by my personal attendance my own grateful recollection of His Majesty's past kindness and condescension, I would most gladly avail myself of it.

   I have the honour to remain,
         Sir,
         Your most faithful and obedient Servant,
               J RUSSELL
               His Excellency, M Guizot, Minister of Foreign Affairs.

As a result of this letter, the King of the French sent a donation of ten guineas through his Ambassador in London, the Count de St Aulaire, to whom Russell replied:

> Canterbury, Nov 22 1844

Sir,

Your Excellency will have had an official acknowledgement of Ten Guineas received by the Society of Schoolmasters as a Donation from His Majesty the King of the French. But allow me, as Treasurer, to add an expression of thanks, which I tender to His Majesty with all respect, and unfeigned sincerity; and request you will assure His Majesty, that the Queen of England has no subjects more sensible of kindness, or more grateful for benefits conferred, than the Members of the Society whose pride it is to have the King's honoured name upon their Rolls, while they enjoy the renewed conviction that they are not forgotten by His Majesty.

> I have the honour to be, etc,
>> J RUSSELL
>>> To His Excellency the French Ambassador

The following year St Aulaire wrote again to Russell:

> Hertford House
> 23 April 1845

Sir,

It affords me much pleasure to have to inform you of a fresh proof of the interest His Majesty the King of the French takes in the welfare of the 'Schoolmasters' Society'. His Majesty grants a Donation of £50 which I have the honour to forward to you enclosed.

> I am, Sir,
> Your obedient Servant,
>> ST AULAIRE

Russell replied on 10 April 1845 in similar vein to his letter above.

Appendix IV
The Vacation and Annotations, 1817

Sung at the Anniversary meetings of the Society of Schoolmasters:

Air - The Roast Beef of Old England

I

I sing of those Sages of fame and desert,
Professors of Science and Masters of Art,
Who learning, and morals, and wisdom impart
  To all our fine Youths of Old England,
   And who give them Old English Roast Beef.

II

Our labours, our pleasures, our joy, and our care,
Our plagues and our pastimes now let us compare,
Like other poor mortals, we have a full share;
  But we have the Roast Beef of Old England,
   We divide the Old English Roast Beef.

Air - A Begging we will go

III

Vacation now approaches,
How charming is the view!
In chaises, gigs, and coaches,
New pleasures we'll pursue.
  And a roving we will go, etc.

IV

From scanning musty pages
We fly on airy wing;
Like birds let loose from cages,
We soar aloft, and sing.
  And a roving, etc.

V

We view, with magnifying hope,
Our coffers overflow;
And then invert the telescope
In viewing what we owe.
     And a roving, etc,

VI

Then welcome festive wit and song,
And welcome mirth and glee;
In parties gay, both night and day,
From care and fagging free.
     And a roving, etc.
     And a sporting we will go.

Air - Since then I'm doom'd

VII

But soon we're doom'd a sad reverse to mourn,
This fleeting Moon already wanes apace;
And we to Gerund-grinding must speedily return,
Where Bills till now unthought-of stare us in the face,
Black Monday's feeble muster slow comfort too imparts,
This Moulting-time will break our tender hearts.

Air - The Lads of Lower Ormond

VIII

Indeed the first week is the worst in the year,
E'en Boys, like their Masters, now drooping appear;
With Mothers dictating about their spoil'd Sons,
Or, instead of new Scholars, we see but old Duns.

Air - The Roast Beef of Old England

IX

This gloom soon dispels, and we take to the gear,
The School fills apace, and the Duns disappear;
Here's a promising crop, and a fig for all fear -
     We shall soon have another Vacation,
     Aye, and two Honey-moons ev'ry year.

X

To wake the bright soul, and give intellect day,
Is a duty divine, we're now call'd to obey;
An honour with HOMER and MILTON to stray
Through the groves of the great Academus,
As ORLEANS so nobly can say.

Air - The Yellow-Hair'd Laddie

XII

But man's doom'd to sorrow, whate'er his success,
While union and friendship his sorrows make less;
The Widow and Orphan our union shall bless,
While we're blest in drying the tear of distress.

XIII

From the arrows of Fortune no prudence can fly:
But Sympathy follows, her balm to apply,
With kindness to soothe, and bounty to cheer,
As the dew falls from Heav'n to gladden the year.

Air - Aileen Aroon

Still more happy tidings the Widow shall here,
For now Royal Sympathy wipes off the tear:
    A new Constellation bright
    Rises to cheer our sight;
Kindling kind virtue and shedding propitious light
The Bright Stars of Brunswick all-glorious appear!

ANNOTATIONS

(a) The Society of Schoolmasters was established in 1798 for the benefit of decayed Members, their Widows and Orphans. It is composed of the Masters of Endowed Schools and Boarding Schools; but relief is extended to distressed Ushers and other persons connected with the profession. Hence the Charitable Branch of the Institution is supported by Public Subscription, and is liberally patronised by many eminent characters. The Anniversaries are numerously attended, and the present Song was composed for the occasion at an early period of the Society. It has been sung by several Professional Singers; and at the last Anniversary (1816) the company requested that it might be printed. Similar requests, however, had been frequently refused; but the inducement for complying at present is the opportunity which the publication affords of preserving the copy of a most interesting Letter, which forms the subject of the next note.

(b) '*As Orleans so nobly can say*'. This verse has been recently introduced, with a view of commemorating in the Society a circumstance well worthy of being recorded.

That HOMER, MILTON, and other great Poets and Philosophers, were School-masters is well understood; but that a Royal Duke and young Military Hero of great promise should have been a Member of the Profession is extraordinary. The fact, however, has been communicated in the following authentic manner.

Prince LOUIS-PHILIP, DUKE OF ORLEANS, having been invited to dine at the late Anniversary of the Society of Schoolmasters, wrote a letter from his house at Twickenham, regretting his inability to attend, but enclosing at the same time a liberal donation to the Charity. His Serene Highness was pleased to add, 'That among the motives which made him feel an attachment to Schoolmasters, was that of having been himself once a Member of the Profession. It was one of the many vicissitudes of fortune which had fallen to his lot, that at a period of severe distress and persecution, he had the good luck of being admitted as Teacher in a College, where he gave lessons regularly for the space of eight months. He hoped, therefore, that the Society for the Relief of Distressed Schoolmasters would permit him to tender his mite as a fellow Schoolmaster'.

The particulars of the above, with other interesting circumstances relating to the DUKE OF ORLEANS, may be seen in *Tweddell's Remains*, recently published (p. 41); where it is stated, in substance, that this accomplished Prince, born to the richest patrimony of perhaps any subject in the world, and eventually Heir to a great Monarchy, was in the year 1793 a wandering emigrant in the Alps, in danger and distress; until (as before noticed) he obtained an asylum, as Teacher of the Mathematics, at a College near Coire, in Switzerland. It is added, that he gained the appointment, against competitors, by superior merit, for his rank was not known; and that he discharged the duties of his new office with the highest honour.

The affecting narrative concluded thus (p.44): 'With the same purity of morals and greatness of soul, he was seen, at sixteen years of age, a Prince without pride; a General at seventeen, three times rallying his troops at Gemappe; a Professor of Geometry at twenty, as if he had consecrated many years to the study of the Sciences; and every where, in all circumstances, he appeared as if born for the station which he filled'. It may be remarked, that the subject of the foregoing note is not only singularly interesting, but highly edifying. It affords a noble example of fortitude and magnanimity under the severest trials of fortune; and a fine illustration to youth of the importance of those early acquirements which fortune cannot take away. The story must ever command a distinguished place in the annals of illustrious characters.

(c) 'The Widow and Orphan our union shall bless'. This early prediction has been happily verified, and a foundation laid for its permanent accomplishment.

The above line also alludes to the circumstances, that, before the Society was formed, no plan of general association existed in this country among Schoolmasters, notwithstanding the laudable example of other professions. The utility of the present Establishment has been already experienced in various ways, even by the more prosperous Members of the Society. Besides the gratification of relieving and protecting distressed individuals and families, much pleasure and advantage must flow from professional communication and friendly intercourse. In short, the Institution is at once calculated to promote the honour and interest of the Profession, the advancement of learning, and the cause of humanity.

(d) 'Bright Stars of Brunswick'. This verse was added in grateful commemoration of the support rendered to the Institution by different branches of our Royal Family. First by the DUKE OF CAMBRIDGE, who graciously condescended to become the Patron of the Society in the year 1811; and since by the liberal aid and eloquence of his Royal Brothers, the DUKES OF KENT and SUSSEX, who, in his absence, have presided at the anniversaries with great advantage to the Charity.

Appendix V
Presidents, Chairmen and Venues

PRESIDENTS

1798-1808	The Bishop of Gloucester (G.I. Huntingford)
1808-1832	The Bishop of Hereford (Huntingford, as above)
	The Bishop of Carlisle (S. Goodenough)
1832-1848	The Archbishop of Canterbury (William Howley)
1849-1862	The Archbishop of Canterbury (John Bird Sumner)
1862-1868	The Archbishop of Canterbury (C.T. Longley)
1869-1882	The Archbishop of Canterbury (A.C. Tait)
1883-1896	The Archbishop of Canterbury (Edward White Benson)
1896-1903	The Archbishop of Canterbury (Frederick Temple)
1903-1918	The Bishop of Hereford (J. Percival)
1918-1927	Revd Dr Edwin Abbott
1927-1942	Revd and Hon. E. Lyttleton
1942-1946	Revd G.H. Rendall
1946-1949	Sir Henry Marten
1949-1952	A.E. Conybeare
1952-1962	Sir Claude Elliott
1962-1985	Richard Curtis
1985-1997	John Spencer
1997-	David Skipper

CHAIRMEN

1797-1800	Revd Dr William Barrow
1800-1812	Revd Dr Charles Burney
1813-1821	Revd Dr John Russell
1822-1838	Ven. Archdeacon Charles Parr Burney
1838-1848	Revd Dr John Morris
1848-1852	Revd Dr Edward Rice
1852-1880	Revd Dr Thomas Spyers
1880-1921	Revd Richard Lee
1921-1926	William Rushbrooke
1926-1947	R.F. Cholmeley
1947-1960	R. McArthur
1960-1978	Christopher Evers
1978-1985	John Spencer
1985-1997	David Skipper

1997-2005   Canon Keith Wilkinson
2005-   John Wolters

VENUES

1797-1824   *Crown and Anchor* Tavern
1824-1841   Literary Fund Society's Chambers, 4 Lincoln's Inn Fields
1841-1856   73 Great Russell Street
1856   Rectory House, Devonshire Square
1856-1860   73 Great Russell Street
1860-1872   4 Adelphi Terrace
1872-1879   10 John Street, Adelphi
1879-1889   7 Adelphi Terrace
1889-1891   9 Adelphi Terrace
1891-1905   7 Adelphi Terrace
1905-1921   40 Denison House, Westminster
             (Between 1824 and 1921 these had all been the home of the Literary Fund)
1921-1948   College of Preceptors, Bloomsbury Square
1948-1953   Owen's School, Islington
1954-1963   Gordon House, Gordon Square
1963-1998   United Westminster Schools, 53 Palace Street
1998-2002   Westminster School
2002-   SGBI, Chislehurst

Appendix VI
Schools Connected with the Society

Many schools have contributed to the Society through annual subscriptions or regular collections. Many more individuals who attended or worked in these, and other, schools have benefited from the Society, as have their dependants. Several such beneficiaries had gone on to work in the considerable number of small private schools only to be hit by illness, the growth of Board schools or war. After the First World War contributions from individual schools declined, possibly because it was thought the state was providing sufficient help or that HMC and IAPS were making donations on their behalf. In fact state aid did not solve the problems of the poor and the contributions of HMC were erratic (if not stingy) though those of IAPS were both more generous and consistent. It remains true that those teaching children up to the ages of 11 or 13 have been less well protected by pensions schemes. The list below contains some of the schools, past and present, linked in some way to the Society. It is not intended to be more than a 'snap shot' for there is scarcely a school in the independent sector which does not feature in our records. Some of those included may just bring back memories!

Abingdon
Aldenham
Alleyns
Allhallows
Amersham
Archbishop Holgate's, York
Arnold, Blackpool
Ashby de la Zouche GS
Ashville
Audlem GS
Audley House School
Aysgarth School
Bancrofts
Barnard Castle
Barnsley GS
Barnstaple GS
Batley GS
Beacon School, Sevenoaks
Beccles GS
Bede School, Sunderland
Bedford School
Bedford Modern

Berkhamsted
Bethany School
Bideford GS
Birkenhead
Bishop Stortford
Bloxham
Blue Coat School, Birmingham
Blundells
Boston GS
Bradfield
Bradford GS
Brentwood, Essex
Brigg GS
Brighton College
Bristol GS
Bromsgrove
Bungay GS
Carlisle GS
Charterhouse
Chatham House
Cheadle Hulme
Cheltenham

Cheltenham Prep
Chichester GS
Chigwell
Christ Church Cathedral School, Oxford
Christ's Hospital
Churchers
City of London
Claremont House School
Claughton Prep
Clifton College
Cockermouth School
Coleraine Academical Institution
Colfe's
Coopers
Cranbrook
Cranleigh
Crypt
Dame Allan's
Darlington GS
Daventry GS
Dartmouth High School
Denstone
Devonport High School
Doncaster GS
Douai
Dover
Downsend, Leatherhead
Downside
Dulwich College
Dulwich College Prep
Dungannon Royal
Durham
Durham Cathedral School
Eagle House
Eastbourne
Edgbaston High School
Edgeborough
Edinburgh Academy
Elizabeth College, Guernsey
Eltham
Emanuel
Epsom
Eton
Exeter
Farnham GS
Felsted
Fettes
Forest
Framlingham
Friends' School, Saffron Walden
Frome GS
George Watsons

Giggleswick
Glasgow High School
Godolphin
Grenville College
Gresham's School, Holt
Grove House, Tunbridge Wells
Grove Park School, Wrexham
Haberdashers Aske
Haileybury
The Hall, Sunderland
Harrow
Haverford West GS
Hereford Cathedral School
Heriot Watt
Hexham GS
Highgate
Holmefield School, Sutton
Homesdale, Westerham
Hurstpierpoint
Hutton GS
Hymers School, Hull
Ilminster GS
Ipswich
Kelly College
Kelvinside Academy
Kettering GS
Kimbolton
KES, Bath
KES, Birmingham
KES, Camp Hill
KES, Stourbridge
KES, Witney
King Edward VI, Chelmsford
King Edward VI GS, Southampton
King Edward VI, Stratford on Avon
King Edward VII, Sheffield
King Henry VIII, Coventry
Kings Bruton
Kings College Choir School, Cambridge
Kings College School, Wimbledon
Kings School, Canterbury
Kings School, Chester
Kings, Gloucester
Kings, Grantham
Kings, Macclesfield
Kings, Rochester
Kings, Taunton
Kings, Tynemouth
Kings, Worcester
Kings Lynn GS
Kingsland Grange
Kingston GS

Kingswood
King William's, Isle of Man
Kneller Hall Military School of Music
Latymer Upper
Lavenham GS
Leeds GS
Lewes GS
Linlithgow House School, Croydon
Liverpool College
Liverpool Institute
Llandaff Cathedral School
Llandovery
Loretto
Loughborough GS
Louth GS
Lucton
Magdalen College School
Maidstone GS
Malvern
Manchester GS
Marlborough
Mercers
Merchant Taylors', Crosby
Merchant Taylors', Northwood
Mill Hill
Monkton Coombe
Monmouth
Morpeth GS
Morrison's Academy
The Mount School, Exeter
New College Choir School, Oxford
North London Collegiate School
Northallerton Prep
Northampton GS
Norwich School
Oakham
Old Hall, Ware
Old Hall, Wellington, Shropshire
Oswestry
Oundle
Owen's School, London
Owen's School, Manchester
Oxford Boys High School
Palmers
Parmiters
Penrith GS
Perse
Petersfield GS
Plymouth College
Pocklington
Portora, Enniskillen
Portsmouth GS

Queen's College, Taunton
Queen's School, Basingstoke
Queenswood
QEGS, Barnet
QEGS, Blackburn
QEGS, Wakefield
Radley
Ratcliffe
Reading School
Reading Junior School
Redruth GS
Repton
Richmond GS
Ripon Cathedral School
RGS, Colchester
RGS, Guildford
RGS, Lancaster
RGS, Worcester
Rossall
Royal High School, Edinburgh
Royal Hospital School, Holbeach
Royal Masonic School, Bushey
Royal School, Dungannon
Royal School, Enniskillen
Rugby
Ruthin
Rutlish
Rydal
Ryde, Isle of Wight
St Albans
St Andrew's, Eastbourne
St Bede's, Eastbourne
St Bees
St Dunstan's
St Edmund's, Canterbury
St Edmund's, Ware
St Edward's, Oxford
St James' School, Grimsby
St John's, Leatherhead
St Mary's, Calne
St Michael's, Tenbury
St Olave's
St Paul's School
St Paul's Cathedral Choir School
St Peter's, York
Salisbury Cathedral School
Salisbury School
Scarborough
Seaford
Sedbergh
Sevenoaks
Shebbear

Sherborne
Shrewsbury
Silcoates
Sir William Turner's
Sittingborne GS
Stamford
Stockport GS
Sutton Valence
Swansea GS
Sydenham High School
Taunton School
Temple Grove
Tettenhall
Thetford GS
Tonbridge School
Towcester School
Trent
Trinity School, Croydon
Truro Cathedral School
Truro School
University College School
Uppingham
Usk GS
Victoria College, Jersey
Warminster

Warwick
Wellesley House
Wellingborough
Wellington College
Wellington School, Somerset
Wells Cathedral School
Wells House
Wem GS
West Buckland
Westminster City School
Westminster School
Wigan GS
Wigton GS
Wimbledon College
Wimborne GS
Winchester Cathedral School (Pilgrims')
Winchester College
Windlesham House
Wokingham GS
Wolverhampton GS
Woodbridge
Woodhouse Grove
Worcester Cathedral School
Wyggeston
Wymondham

Notes

1. Beginnings, pp.1-10.

1. Strype, B., quoted in P. Cunningham, *Hand-Book of London* (1850), iv, p.117.
2. *Burke's Correspondence*, Volume IV, p.448.
3. Minutes of Committee, January 1797.
4. *Ibid.*
5. K. Baker, *The Prime Ministers* (1995), p58.
6. Letter from Barrow to Pitt, 7 December 1797.
7. Letter from Barrow to Pitt, 8 December 1797.
8. *Ibid.*
9. *Ibid.*
10. *Ibid.*
11. Report of Meeting with Pitt recorded in Minutes, January 1798.
12. *Ibid.*
13. *Ibid.*
14. For comparative prices/salaries etc., see Further Information, pp.93-6.
15. Rule 14: 18 January 1798.
16. *Ibid.*
17. Appeal letter, 5 December 1802, written by P. Kelly, Secretary and Treasurer.
18. Minutes, 11 February 1809.

2. A Little Over-Confidence?, pp.11-16.

1. Minutes of Committee, 19 September 1807.
2. Minutes, 19 May 1804.
3. Minutes of Extra-Committee Meeting, 5 April 1817.
4. Minutes, 10 November 1809.
5. Minutes, 17 September 1808.
6. Minutes, 19 March, 1808.
7. Minutes, 11 February 1809.
8. Minutes, 19 November 1808.
9. Minutes, 18 March 1809.
10. Minutes, 17 September 1808.
11. Farington Diary, 20 December 1804.
12. Diary of the Revd William Jones.
13. Vincent was, in 1803, Headmaster of Westminster and Vice-President of the Society.
14. Reported in several papers and also on papers for AGM, 1809.
15. J.A. Tregelles: *A History of Hoddesdon.*

3. Dr Kelly and Growing Problems, pp.17-21.

1. Committee circular to members, 7 January 1813.
2. Letter in reply to circular, January 1813.

115

3. Sub-committee report to Committee, 7 June 1817.
4. Minutes, AGM, 22 December 1813.
5. Circular to members, 21 December 1818.
6. Minutes of Extraordinary Committee Meeting, 7 June 1817.
7. *Ibid.*
8. Fairman.
9. Kirkpatrick.
10. Report of Actuaries for Royal Exchange and Atlas Offices, 1818.
11. Committee circular to members, 21 December 1818.
12. *Ibid.*
13. Letter from Morgan to Kelly, 27 November 1818.
14. Committee circular to members, 21 December 1818.

4. LIFE AND DEATH: THE COLLAPSE OF THE LIFE FUND, pp.22-8.
1. Minutes, AGM, 22 December 1818.
2. Trollope's letter to Committee, 23 January 1819.
3. Sub-committee report, 6 February 1819.
4. Morgan, letter to the Committee, 27 February 1819.
5. Morgan, letter to the Committee, 6 March 1819.
6. Extraordinary Committee Meeting, 9 December 1820.
7. *Ibid.*
8. Assurers calculated risk on a scale known as the Northampton Bills of Mortality.
9. Morgan, letter to the Committee, 26 March 1821.
10. Extraordinary Committee Meeting, 10 March 1821.
11. Letter, 29 December 1813.

5. THE CHARITABLE FUND, pp.29-32.
1. Minutes, AGM, 22 December 1814.
2. Kelly: Circular to all members, 29 September 1820.
3. Report to the Committee, 21 March 1818.
4. Report of the sub-committee, 3 April 1819.
5. *Ibid.*
6. *Ibid.*
7. *Ibid.*
8. *Ibid.*
9. Extraordinary General Meeting, 21 June 1821.

6. ROYAL SUPPORT, pp.33-40.
1. Committee Meeting Minutes, 1 February 1823.
2. Committee Meeting Minutes, 3 December 1825.
3. Cases, 4 December 1824.
4. *Ibid.*
5. J.H. Plumb, *The First Four Georges*, Batsford (1956), pp.150-1.
6. Letter, Anson to Russell, 6 September 1849.
7. *Ibid.*
8. Russell's reply to Anson, 8 September 1849.
9. *Ibid.*; dinners had ceased in 1833 and the Duke of Kent had died in 1820.
10. Letter, Russell to Phipps, 24 July 1850.
11. Phipps' reply to Russell, 30 July 1850.
12. Letter, Duc d'Orleans to Kelly, 15 March 1817.
13. For a fascinating account, see Owen Chadwick's *Victorian Miniature* (1960).
14. *The Story of the Governesses' Benevolent Institution*, Grange Press (1962) for private circulation, p.9.
15. *Ibid.*

7. A REMARKABLE GROUP OF MEN, pp.41-9.
1. Owen Chadwick, *The Victorian Church Part 1*, A&C Black (1966), p.235.

2. See Francis Doyle quoted in David Newsome, *Godliness and Good Learning*, Murray (1961), p.49.
3. Chadwick, *op. cit.*, p.453.
4. Chadwick, *op. cit.*, p.452.
5. Chadwick, *op. cit.*, p.134.
6. Asa Briggs, *Victorian People*, Odhams (1954) p.149, quoting a Rugby Housemaster in 1829.
7. Asa Briggs, *op. cit.*, p.152.
8. A.R. Ashwell and R.G. Wilberforce, *Life of Samuel Wilberforce* (1880).
9. See Chadwick, *The Victorian Church*, p.133.
10. Newsome, *op. cit.*, p.36.
11. Chadwick, *op. cit.*, p.198.

8. A Degree of Adjustment, pp.53-3.
1. Letter from Thomas Morris to Russell, 16 December 1849.
2. Now St Edmund's, Canterbury.
3. Special Committee Meeting, 11 July 1863.
4. Committee Meeting, 3 October 1863.

9. Relief: A Period of Relative Calm, pp.54-8.
1. Minutes, Special Meeting, 10 March 1883.
2. Meeting note, 9 February 1901.
3. Meeting note, 18 October 1902. In 2001, the Society fixed a provisional date for its June meeting as the government had decided to celebrate Queen Elizabeth II's Golden Jubilee on the planned date.
4. Committee Meeting Minutes, 11 October 1913.
5. Letter from COS, 1 April 1903.
6. Letter from the Revd Dr Rendall, 5 November 1905.
7. Minutes, AGM, 6 March 1915.

10. Help!, pp.59-66.
1. Letter from Secretary of Clergy Orphan Corporation to Committee, 6 October 1884.
2. Relief Book, quoted in Minutes, 1 February 1823.
3. Committee meeting, 21 November 1812.
4. Committee meeting, 21 November 1812.
5. Relief Book, p.135.
6. *Op. cit.*, p.28.
7. Relief Book, p.105.
8. *Op. cit.*, p.129.
9. *Op. cit..*, p.131.

11. Tales of Distress and Dishonesty, pp.67-72.
1. *The Times*, October 1866.
2. Letter to Baker, 30 June 1896.
3. Letter sent to all interested parties, this one to A. Roberts of COS, 2 July 1896.
4. *The Times*, 3 and 5 December 1891.
5. *The Times*, 13 April 1892.
6. *The Times*, 22 October 1895.
7. Letter to the Society, 1 November 1899.
8. Letter, 2 November 1899.
9. *Ibid.*
10. *The Times*, 29 December 1899.
11. Relief Book, June 1922.
12. Minutes, 8 December 1928.
13. Minutes, 14 December 1929.
14. Minutes, 9 March 1929.
15. Minutes, 8 October 1932.
16. Meeting, 14 March 1936.

12. DRIFTING TOWARDS CRISIS, pp.73-6.

1. Committee Meeting Minutes, 3 March 1923.
2. Committee Meeting Minutes, 9 March 1935.
3. Committee Meeting Minutes, 9 December 1939.
4. Committee Meeting Minutes, 13 March 1943.
5. Committee Meeting Minutes, 11 March 1943.
6. See Appendices.
7. Quentin Bell, *Bloomsbury Recalled*, Columbia University Press (1995), p.151.

13. CRISIS, pp.77-80.

1. McArthur, 5 June 1947.
2. Letter, G.A. Riding to Secretary, 9 March 1949.
3. AGM, 6 March 1951.
4. Committee Meeting Minutes, 3 October 1950.
5. Committee Meeting Minutes, 6 March 1951.
6. Committee Meeting Minutes, 4 March 1952.
7. Committee Meeting Minutes, 16 September 1952.
8. Chairman's report, 2 March 1954.
9. Letter to Provost of Eton, 10 June 1952.
10. McArthur's report, 8 March 1955.
11. McArthur's report, 3 March 1959.

14. A BRIEF RESPITE, pp.81-4.

1. Berkhamsted School was asked by the President to print the booklet; it declined to do so.
2. Treasurer's (J.S. Smith) report, 5 March 1975.
3. C. Evers, Chairman's report, 6 March 1974.
4. Committee Meeting Minutes, 11 June 1975.
5. Committee Meeting Minutes, 4 December 1975.
6. Letter to the Society, 1981.

15. SALVATION, pp.85-91.

1. Report of sub-committee, 2 February 1978.
2. Letter from President to HM The Queen, 1 March 1979.
3. President Committee Minutes, 8 June 1978.
4. Treasurer's report, 3 March 1994.
5. Treasurer's report, 2 March 1995.
6. *The Times*, obituary, 1919.
7. Report of the President, 14 March 1997.
8. Letter, 28 February 1996 to Committee.
9. Circular received by Committee, 4 March 1982.
10. Chairman, AGM, March 2001.
11. President's report to members, 2002.

Bibliography

Unpublished Papers

The Minute Books of the Society, 1797-2002

Address and Resolutions, 18 January 1798

Rules, Orders and Regulations respecting the Joint Stock of the Society of Schoolmasters, 1802

Rules, Orders and Regulations respecting the Charitable Fund of the Society of Schoolmasters. 1802

Lists of Subscribers, 1801ff

A Subscription of the Family of the Late Mrs Applebee, 1803

Address and Letter of Thomas Hammersley, 1809

Rules and Regulations of the Society of Schoolmasters, 1808

Rules and Regulations of the Society of Schoolmasters, 1813

Letter appealing for subscribers to a fund for P. Kelly and list of such subscribers, 1812-13 and letters in reply.

Address to the Public, 1815

Address to the Public, 1822

The Vacation, 1817

Letters from William Morgan about the Joint Stock Fund 1813ff; Committee Report, 1818; Kelly's Explanations, 1818

Letters to members winding up the Joint Stock Fund and re-establishing the Charitable Fund, 1821

Balloting List for Committee, 1821

Annual Accounts and Reports, 1822-2004

The Alphabetical List of Persons Relieved, c.1830-1929

Secondary Sources

There is a wealth of material covering the period the society has been in existence. These are just a few.

Ackroyd, Peter, *London: The Biography*, Chatto and Windus (2000)

Baker, Kenneth, *The Prime Ministers*, Thames & Hudson (1995)

Bell, Quentin, *Bloomsbury Recalled*, New York (1995)

Briggs, Asa, *Victorian People*, Odhams (1954)

Chadwick, Owen, *The Victorian Church, Parts I and II*, A & C Black (1966)

Chadwick, Owen, *Victorian Miniature*, Hodder & Stoughton (1960)

Farrar, F.W., *Eric; or Little by Little*, London edn (1914)

Hughes, Thomas, *Tom Brown's Schooldays*, Oxford edn (1921)

Newsome, David, *Godliness and Good Learning*, Murray (1961)
Plumb, J.H., *The First Four Georges*, Batsford (1956)
Reader, W.J., *Life in Victorian England*, Batsford (1964)
Royle, Edward, *Modern Britain*, Arnold (1987)
Willey, Basil, *Nineteenth Century Studies*, London (1949)
Williams, E.N., *Life in Georgian England*, Batsford (1962)
Wilson, A.N., *The Victorians*, Hutchinson (2002)

Index

Page numbers in **bold** refer to illustrations.